PHIL CALLAHAN

AN INTERVIEW WITH JOE BLANKINSHIP

Transcribed by Lee Bracker

PHIL CALLAHAN EXPLAINS OUR WORLD BASED ON PARAMAGNETISM in an intense introspective discussion with Joe Blankinship. Topics include weak electromagnetic fields, World War II, and agriculture

For information contact: lbracker@hotmail.com

Print On Demand by
Lulu Publishing
www.lulu.com

Cover design by Lee Bracker

Printed in the United States of America

Library of Congress Cataloging-in-Publication Data not available yet.

Bracker, Lee.

Phil Callahan – An Interview With Joe Blankinship

ISBN 978-0-557-99307-9 (trade pbk.)

1. Paramagnetics. 2. World War II. 3. Agriculture. 4. Natural Cures

5. Entomology 6. Radio Technology 7. Infra Red Technology I. Title.

PART ONE

Joe and Marilyn Blankinship visit with Philip and Winnie Callahan at their home in Albuquerque, New Mexico in 2004. A few initial minutes of introduction are not captured on video.

As if you just entered the room you're instantly engaged with the conversation taking place. The content and dynamics of their time together is captured in this perfect example of both men's recollections of their lives and research.

The transcription from video tape to print is an attempt to preserve the charm of their candid conversational style and is presented intact as much as possible. Where there is editing of words and phrases it is only done for the purpose of clarity or to make sense. The decision was made to not interfere with the fluidity of the "read" with indications as to where these modifications occur.

Phil Callahan has published eighteen books; many of them touched upon and shared in this visit. The transcription from video to print was completed late July of 2010 at the request of Joe Blankinship whose aim is to carry Dr. Philip Callahan's legacy generations forthcoming.

Enjoy the ride!

Tape begins

Joe: ... and cell phone exposure will sterilize eggs and they won't hatch. Bill Bailey, who worked for Motorola, said, "They don't sell many cellphones to chickens and peacocks." That was his answer to that. But we've still got them. I found that if you take a little möbius and put it with a little magnetite in a disk and squeeze them it disrupts direct EMFs. Tesla came up with this purple disk. I gave you one or two of them.. they had the cobalt and aluminum in them, the yin and the yang. When you combine the disk and a little möbius, it keeps the rays from penetrating the skull. To make it, the disk must be placed on a bed of granite and exposed to a high voltage Tesla coil for about a day. We're putting them on a polar concentrator.. six and a half million co-factor..

Phil: (Takes out a small statue from his pocket) He took the Virgin Mary similar to this one and filled it with magnetite and sealed it. He hasn't had a problem again. I've got the Virgin Mary and filled it with paramagnetic rock. (**Holds up a small statue of the Virgin Mary from his pocket to show Marilyn**). It works for the common cold and I've never even had a sniffle.

Joe: This doctor Marshall.. I handed you his name there, is very concerned. I gave him a copy of the time you did the interview in Nexus Magazine about the cancer that you had and other people and so forth. I also told him that you were able to successfully treat leprosy. I went into detail about it and he is very interested in that. He's thinking that everyone that I have ever told about taking magnetite by spoonful think that it's an herb and it won't actually dissolve.. it won't actually go in, but it's actually doing something.

Phil: As it goes into you, it puts energy into your body. It's a quick cure, actually.

Joe: A doctor in Tucson I was talking to, Dr. Best, bought an infrared box that people can get into and gave them the paramagnetics. They swallow it down and then get in the box. Do you remember the fellow in Pink Polk, Florida, Roy Davis with all these dogs? He had 200 dogs. Half of them had cancer and the other half were the control group. The half that he fed magnetite to and had sleep on magnetic beds all healed. Every one of the damn dogs. The others that were in the control group, every one of them died.

Phil: I played with chemicals that I had to synthesize for six years when I had a job at Louisiana State University and I got lung cancer. I cured it in less than a month. It was gone inside of a month by taking a teaspoon of magnetite.

Joe: You told me about the pads you made that trace back to the Jewish tradition.

Phil: Yeah, the Shatnez. Nobody knew the name of it until I met this 91 year old Rabbi. He said that it is the Jewish name for sackcloth and ashes. Sackcloth and ashes were not for penance, they were to heal leprosy. When they put sackcloth Hemp and ashes on a leper, it would heal them. It did not have anything to do with penance. In the Bible, they had to do penance and they were healed.

Joe: That was a very important factor that you told me. In fact, I made hundreds of pads like that and I gave them to two hospices. The doctors would come a long and throw them in the garbage can. The nurses would take them back out of the garbage can and give them to the patients. They said they used less narcotics.. no sales!

Phil: Of course.

Joe: Now I found you can benefit these by putting them in a plastic bag, seal them real tight and put them in the freezer. Then when they come back out, they slowly give off energy. There is a change in the CGS when they get back to ambient temperature.

Phil: You actually have some movement.

Joe: So that goes right back to Wilhelm Reich. Wilhelm Reich came to Tucson and had the orgone. I think orgone and paramagnetics are the same thing.

Phil: Of course. That was his name for it. He had to call it something. He didn't know a lot of physics and he had to call it something. So he called the energy, Orgone, but it is the same thing.

Joe: Now he wrote that book "Pathology Cancer" and he got in trouble. That's when they put him in prison and he died just before his release date.

Phil: They put him in jail. That was the American Medical Association doing. I never had much use for them and I still don't. They're as crummy as ever on something like this. It's all greed.

Joe: Money. It's all about money. I've got another thing I have been playing with that I want to tell you about. I read Dr. Paul Langévin where he put crystals between two plates and would tap them to get the coherent wave. When you were talking about the fellow that worked on the radio, you mentioned Langévin at one time. I had a helluva time finding out about him. Langévin made sonar and radar by tapping crystals under pressure. So I made a bunch of stainless steel plates. I put these little magnetite balls in between them and squeezed them. They benefited plants, they benefited animals.

Phil: Plants grow like crazy.

Joe: It's unbelievable. Now, I went a step further. I got a hold of a hyperberic chamber from Bruce Halstead and brought it over to Tucson. It saved my brother's leg. My brother had diabetes. We put him in the chamber three or four times a week.

Phil: Paramagnetic oxygen.

Joe: Paramagnetic oxygen is what it was I found out with, Langévin, I didn't have to put them in a steel plate. I mixed them with sodium silicate and put the stuff together in little balls. I squeezed them up like the holy balls in India. While they were still wet, I squeezed them under tremendously high pressure with the oxygen inside the chamber. They came out of that chamber active and alive. They have paramagnetism. These do not.

Phil: They have oxygen which is paramagnetic.

Joe: They are paramagnetic, but these don't measure on the CGS meter as much as the others.

Phil: They feel warm too.

Joe: They are always warm. There was an old con artist I met years ago in Florida who was selling oxygenated water. He called it "Fountain of Youth Water" from silicon dioxide and ferrous oxide rich source. He made a lot of money, got into trouble with the federal government, moved to Hawaii and they found him over there. Then he moved to Vienna. He buys these balls from me. He's got them on the Internet as "cosmic balls". He sells these damn balls for $30.00 a piece and getting rich. I'm nearly giving them away. The balls do work. I put them in the skimmers of swimming pools which helps to restructure the water. There is a Japanese guy named Dr. Masaru Emoto as well as a few other people who have taken pictures of structured water after they chill it. When they chill it, you can see all these crystallizations and the beautiful forms. They are even talking to the water and if they pray over it, the crystals are pretty. If they speak the words, "Adolf Hitler" or "rock-and-roll", the crystals go to hell. He also studied frozen water crystalline structure.

Phil: It's funny how the human language puts negative words to things that are crummy.

Joe: I spent a lot of time with, Dr. Robert Ricketts, who was an orthodontist.. a really bright man, and even went to Hawaii with him. He wrote a dozen really good books which included hundreds of articles. He worked on Loren Bacall's face by adjusting her jaw to make it perfect. He did a job on Sophia Loren too. Bacall goes on record condemning cosmetic surgery just to get an edge, but anyway, he used the golden ratio. He even made a simple adjustable measuring instrument that looks like a drafters compass, but with three legs instead of two, to measure facial proportions relative to "beauty". I've still got a handmade Fibonacci compass he gave to me. Ricketts was selling vitamins out of a company he had called Morganics Research. So, we got into vitamin deals with him. I bought a sonic grinder. I got it from a copier toner company that went broke who were grinding up the black iron to make the toner. I was selling them the iron they used for the toner. Well, that's pretty well controlled by large companies. There are just a few people who they allow to make money on it because they are getting $80.00 or $90.00 for a little tube. He was making it cheaper and they kind of squeezed him out. When he went bankrupt, I bought the $40,000 sonic grinder for a fraction of its value. So, Morganics Research was coming down and the old man was having me grind up his vitamins and minerals because they retained the crystalline structure. When you beat or grind them and then blend them all together the integrity of the individual crystal is lost. So, now I'm taking quartz and grinding them this way. That's what this Dr. Marshall from Round Tree Research in Texas told me. I have people from all over the world coming by two or three days a week. I don't even have a telephone at my lab. I have people from Germany and China finding me. The natural form of gold is unaltered and alive, organic if you like, until arsenic, mercury, and radium come into contact and kills it. You know, arsenic can be neutralized using magnetite. I've got no formal education nor credibility in all this. It's the things that I am telling them about what you know. They should sell a bunch of your books. Anyway, I think this is your greatest work you have ever written.

Phil: I'm going to write another one pretty soon.

Joe: I'm real into it. Now, Christopher Bird, he died. I went to his funeral where about 200 people showed up. I didn't know that he had a twin either and when his brother came in.. I tell you, that was a jolt.

Phil: I saw a picture of his brother once and they look exactly the same.

Joe: He showed up at the funeral in Georgia. He's doing a book, but Bird books are not well known.. people would be healthier if these books were read. The world ignores him.. even today. Anyway, he had it down to about the last chapter. His wife, Shana, I don't know if she's ever going to do anything with the book, but I would like to get his manuscript from her and and let you finish the last chapter.

Phil: Sure, I would be glad to. He was working on that book back when I knew him, back when I taught in Pittsburgh, he had it about half written then.

Joe: I read the whole book. I went all the way through it. I am down to the last chapter or so and it's really a good book. I can't think of anyone in the world that could do a better job of finishing it than you. I think it would outsell his "Secrets of Plants", "Secret of Soil", or his dowsing book. The water book with your paramagnetics could save the whole damned world.

Phil: Yeah, I could finish it.

Joe: I'll tell Shana about that. Now, the same thing happened with Dr. Benza in Canada. Benza was working on what he called Pima Water. It was phototonic implemented "agua". He was taking iron oxide, putting it in a silicon dioxide pyrex tube and shooting it with a laser through the pyrex and then let the water run over it. He was doing a real good sanitation job using this process. He fine tuned it enough that he could actually take salt out of water.

Phil: I don't know why conventional scientists will not pick up on anything like that. It's too way out for them, but it works. They are beginning to use laser for a few things like that.

Joe: I'm getting old, but I'm going to try to make it up to Alberta and see if I can get his wife to let me take his last notes and see if I can get somebody like you to revise his last notes.

Phil: She's still alive?

Joe: She's still alive. She was a lot younger than us. You know this old man, don't you? I'm slowing down and have to go faster to get our of reverse. It's hell getting old. So much yet to discover.

Phil: Yeah, I know the feeling too well.

Joe: Benza used the electron microscope and measured things. He was doing the same thing that Reich and Rife were doing. And so was Galant Nasion in Canada. Dr. Benza's work is so real like the reality of paramagnetics.

Phil: Wilhelm Reich started all of his stuff, but he wasn't a physicist, so he didn't know much about what he was doing. Funny, it always worked.

Joe: Well, if it works, why change it? These people went into optic electron microscopes and you went into a pinhole camera. Every one of these people that I ever talked to, including Christopher Bird, all believed in dowsing.

Phil: Sure, you have to. They would be crazy if they didn't.

Joe: They would not go talking to the outside public without that. Ben Arbogast, a retired realtor from Tucson, he calls here every once in a while, he's looking for treasure and that kind of stuff, but I'm looking for things that heal. We took the iron oxide and mixed it with lignites and then set it near plants. They registered 800-900 percent more vitamins and minerals.

Phil: That's how it works. If you put paramagnetism in your body, it makes all your vitamins and everything else work 10 times better. You'll never get sick.

Joe: Well, this doctor who's in trouble in New York is a medical doctor doing a different treatment for cancer. He was taking aloe vera, magnetizing it and various other things, and then injecting the aloe vera juice right into the cancer with success. He got into trouble for breaking the Feinstein Act, cancer, cut and burn therapies. He'll get jailed same way Jerry Vail did.

Phil: They never could get me on that because they're afraid of me. I had way too much proof.

Joe: I think they think they're going to outlive us both. You've come out a time or two. I used to ask you a question and you would say, "Joe, your gonna get us both in Alcatraz."

Phil: They're afraid of me. That's the problem. Proof.

Joe: Ben has run into some of these measuring devices that he's playing around with. He's talked to some of these people that he has run into at dowsing meetings. He's coming up with a Bovis measurement. What do you think of Dr. Bovis?

Phil: Antoine Bovis goes back to the wine industry measuring sugar content of grapes. It helped them make better wine and more of it. He did energy research on the great pyramids in the thirties.

Joe: It goes all the way back to Bosie in India.

Phil: He was a famous physicist.

Joe: He was first and right on. He has been responsible for saving millions of people in India.. even has a world recognized university named after him. The man studied the stars. Bosie was knighted by the Queen of England.

Phil: Yes, he got recognized by the Queen.

Joe: He was very good. They have some of his books at the University of Arizona Special Collections. But they won't let me copy them. They said the copier would fade them.

Phil: The copier passes ultraviolet light and they're afraid to use old manuscripts on the copy machine.

Joe: So I have hand copied a lot. He was using a wheatstone bridge. He came pretty close to your machine a hundred years before.

Phil: His was a CGS instrument, but more primitive because they didn't have the transistors back then. They probably could have made a better one if they used mica and peanut vacuum tubes. They had them back then. The first one I made used peanut tubes. They were regular tubes but small. I made one in World War II. I just got a call from the CIA last week. I'm going to get regulation for my work. That surprised me, 60 years later.

Joe: Halstead. They put him in jail for his cancer therapies. But, once he got in, they made him start working on the CIA and Naval Strategic Service for big weapons. They were taking these poisons from poisonous and venomous plants and fish and mixing them with DMSO. They asked him how to kill honey bees. I have lots of his notes. One of the things he was working on during the last part of his life was he was taking the frequencies of the poisons and recording them on disks and broadcasting them beneath regular food. The wrong frequency based on the poison was enough to kill a person.

Phil: Sure, frequencies is what kills. You could make a frequency to kill anybody.

Joe: All good things can be reversed. Reich called orgone two ways.. beneficial orgone that we are familiar with and detrimental orgone that would pass bad vibes.

Phil: Sure..

Joe: Do you realize what this could do to the medical profession with aspirin bottles and other things? If you put arsenic or cyanide in the frequencies, plus you would never even break the bottle.

Phil: No, you would put the toxic frequency in the aspirin and they would never figure out how you were killed.

Joe: Now, Halstead here, during the last part of his life, was using oil of camphor and camphor spirits with DMSO. He was rubbing them right on the lymphatic glands. He was getting tremendous results. The last part of his life, he was injecting them directly into the tumors and he was stimulating the immune system right where the cancers were. Halstead mixed some finely ground magnetite with hydrogen peroxide and injected it right into the area. Finally, he was using DMSO as the vehicle to absorb it through the skin.

Phil: There are a lot of doctors who surreptitiously discover cures. Most doctors when they read my book, they say that's great. If they go ahead and do it, they won't let the American Medical Association know it, of course. It's never widespread knowledge.

Joe: When the FDA ordered his DMSO Handbook burned, I went over there before they did and collected all the hard and soft book copies plus everything else I could. I got several of his unpublished books out of there. They would have been lost forever.

Phil: Halstead was an incredible man. It's a shame the world won't see that body of work.

Joe: What is so magical about camphor?

Phil: Camphor is a plant. It's a scent actually. It's like perfume healing. The scent has valuable healing properties like Frankincense and Myrrh. Of course the perfumers know that. A lot of them are doing research on different kinds of perfumes that help people treat diarrhea and other conditions.

Joe: Halstead had a whole file on camphor. He said camphor is the main ingredient in tiger balm that comes from China.

Phil: Yeah, tiger balm is mostly camphor.

Joe: It's tremendous. It's big business all over the world particularly in asian countries.

Phil: People in the old days.. women used to buy camphor and rub it on their knees for arthritis. Camphor was used in all of the old healing. Then, along came chemical healing which is poison based. It kind of did away with all of the natural healing. But it's coming back now. The natural healers are licensed in some states now.

Joe: There are so many people making money in alternative medicine that now a record number of doctors have adopted the practice of recommending second opinions in their office to get in the money.

Phil: They're finally coming along for the money. That's what does it. There's a lot of money in alternative medicine. Allopathy is a form of legitimizing murder.

Joe: Andrew Weil is in Tucson. He was Harvard trained in medicine, but he saw the importance of alternative medicine. So, he got into it. He is making lots of money selling a little newsletter. Every month, he turns out a newsletter that costs fourteen or fifteen dollars a year. And, he has three to four million people a year subscribing to it. I'm not sure you ever thought about that, but you could put together one million little pamphlets of all the things you hove done.

Phil: Yeah, I never was interested in money too much, I don't guess. Money just comes to me when I need it.

Joe: The same with me. And when something works, I go do something else. I just can't stay on one thing. It drives Marilyn crazy, but that's me. It's sort of a "dis-ease" of mine. I lose interest if it's not making any money.. I wish I was a little more business minded.

Phil: I can't either. Once I solve something, I want to go on to something else and try to solve it. That's the problem with life, just keeping ahead. I'm probably going to write a book before too long and it's going to be a hodgepodge of all these things that I have solved.

Joe: I think that would be great, just a bathroom book, just a page or two at a time. The last time I saw Christopher Bird alive was in Sedona. He called me a and said, "I'm going to be in Arizona." I said, "When?" He said, "I'm going to go through Sedona. Joe, I don't feel like going down to that hot country where you are." I said, "I'll come up there." So, I went up there and spent three days with him at Poca Loca. We spent a lot of time together and we talked a lot about you. Your ears were probably burning. He said that you are one of the human beings that write things that a layman could read. Or, even a kid's coloring book. They'll read anything. They don't discriminate and because the technology of truth is so simple, it's interesting to them which carries on throughout a lifetime.

Phil: That's the only way to do it really.

Joe: He said the profession wants to talk in riddles. You are just too frank and too many people can understand what you're saying. I mentioned that people don't read complete books anymore and what about putting the information in little pamphlets. He said he thought that was the coming thing.

Phil: That's what I'm doing now. I'm going back into all this stuff and doing pictures with it. What I learned from the Montauk Project; what I learned form the Philadelphia Experiment; and what I learned from the interplane wing strut; what I learned from the B-26 I flew in World War II when I was decorated and I learned from airplanes. The Wright brothers were incredible people.

Joe: They weren't super educated either.

Phil: They were just bicycle mechanics. One of them saw a piece of paper flying through a barrel one time and that was the beginning of the wind tunnel. He got a barrel and made a wind tunnel. That's how they built their glider.

Joe: There's something I wanted to ask you about. William Lear believed there were UFOs and contact in the country. So did Wilhelm Reich.

Phil: So do I.

Joe: You do? I never talked to you about this. I know two or three people who were high in the military and checked the Roswell incident. I took Wilhelm Reich over to Roswell. He and I went over and look at it. He talked to the rancher and all of the people who were close to this stuff. It was real and they were eye witnesses.

Phil: It was real for sure. The rancher wouldn't lie. He knew what he saw.

Joe: We talked to all these people. When Wilhelm Reich came back, he believed that this country got a lot of data for engineering for switches, computer chips, optic fibers, etc. from ETs. He believed they back engineered this stuff and credited the people they wanted to credit. They got a lot of data out of that exchange. Dr. Einstein got the Nobel Prize for light optics.

Phil: I don't doubt that the transistor came straight from Roswell. No doubt about it. What was the guy's name who invented penicillin? Fleming. He got his ideas from what they found at Roswell. It wasn't mold on bread because the old Jewish Rabbis used moldy dry bread and charcoal as remedies. They were smart. Actually, there is a big round spot of radioactive decay there. There was a lot of this "magic dirt" this one guy called it. It souped up the silver so that it could be used for all kinds of means. I think the transistor came out of that. The transistor is made of silicate doped with iron oxide or doped with radium arsenide, one or the other. You can build them I'm sure. I'm writing up my memoirs now because I got the promise of getting the Medal of Honor for what I did in World War II. All I did to survive was to take a little peanut tube and powered it with paramagnetic rock.

Joe: I took paramagnetics and made my first radio. I took nothing but copper wires and carbon chips. I had a lot of trouble keeping it on a station. I put it together. I found if I put it on a bed of magnetic iron oxide of sand, it worked even better.

Phil: That's the old crystal set that came along when I was a boy. I made my first crystal set. When crystal sets came out, they were nothing but non-linear transistors. You had to search around for the right point.

Joe: It went all the way from that to the vacuum tube and then it went back to that again.

Phil: It went a complete circle back to the crystal. It's all crystal now. Everything is transistorized now. Like that picture of the pyramid of Malcolm. I went to a pyramid named Malcolm's Nest. There was a whole limestone cliff which is diamagnetic. In the pyramid, you will find some other rock that was brought in that was paramagnetic. There is always paramagnetics. If they couldn't find it locally, they would bring it in.

Joe: Halstead told me that in every bird, every homing pigeon, there is a small amount of magnetite in the brain. He told me if you put a tiny magnet on the top of the brain of the bird, the bird becomes lost. He had a degree in toxicology as well as oceanography in addition to medicine. He believed these whales that come in, they are getting disoriented because the magnetism they are getting has been deguaussed.

Phil: Yes, they become sick or something and it deguaussed the magnetism in their brian. They don't know where they're going, so they come ashore. There's no question about that.

Joe: There is a man who went to Sweden years ago and brought a bunch of magnetite back. He breaks it up in little pieces and puts it in little things for people to wear around their neck. He calls it North Star. He has been selling these chips for $50 dollars for years and years. There is just a little tiny chip in there. He sells them to change people's appearance, makes them feel better, makes them feel healthier. He says it makes them lucky at gambling and that crap.

Phil: It won't help with gambling, but it will make them feel better when they lose their money.

Joe: Yeah, it made them feel better after they lost their money.

Phil: You can't win on gambling. The casinos have it set up so you can't win.

Joe: They have a mathematical certainty there. I had a friend who used to work for the airlines. He said they had crashes that would come out around Las Vegas and that other place up there. They had to guard the planes as they were coming in because the people had a lot of money on them. When a plane went down and people were going out of there, there was no one and anything left, not even wrist watches.

Phil: I was talking to a casino guy one time who told me some guy came in there thinking he was smart. He was also looking for magnetism. He could just come in with a paramagnetic rock and mess them up.

Joe: They have spent fortunes, the Ross Club spent about half a million dollars to try to give the people a false sense of security to make them feel good. They experimented with lights. They found that blue and green lights were out.

Phil: They made you too energetic.

Joe: Gold tuned people down. They also found they could put magnetite in various different papers and around the place and found that people were calmer. One thing that Bobo and Mike Schell did was experimentation for NASA. You remember when John Glenn went up then returned with what was called a magnetic deficiency? He busted his head falling down, etc. They found out that all the astronauts that go up now have magnetic oxide inside their suits in order to keep down the deficiency. Linemen, who are working on high voltage electricity, now they are incorporating magnetic iron oxide in their clothing.

Phil: They are all wearing a shatnez now. It is a paramagnetic vest. It stimulates the immune system. It gets your immune system so high that nothing can touch you. Like I said, just carry a paramagnetic rock in our pocket and you would be healthy all your life.

Joe: Once I got your CGS meter on the Arizona rock, then I could go where the quartz and the magnet run together. It went around at eddies, where the water would turn and the heavy parts would fall out. I would mine the stuff right there. At that point, I could get every single one of them and put them in the meter and they would be 19,000 plus.

Phil: Sure, well the meter only went up to forty or something.

Joe: It came by the number ten. The last one that came by said ten magnification. I got a couple of those. I had to clean off the tape before I got that one.

Phil: The first one only went up to 2,000. I got calls back from people, especially out here where the soil is 2,000. They couldn't hardly use it, because it was already at 2,000. So I had to redesign it and bring it up to 40,000 or whatever it is now. I didn't have any trouble changing. I got an electro-engineer who just switched the lead circuits in it. The biggest commercial meters cost $6,000. They said it was because it was so hard to wind the coils. I found out you could send to Germany and get the coils wound for $50.00 each.

Joe: The first one I ever saw was from Patrick Flanagan. He bought it from some German company. He had $6,000 in it. When I got one of yours, it was better than his.

Phil: Mine was a lot better than the commercial ones. Bob Pike was an engineer. He took my circuit design and put it together perfectly.

Joe: Christopher Bird did a story on this. The last thing he was going to do was he was going to put together a water filtration deal. He believed that paramagnetics was the answer to the water.

Phil: When was the date of that trial?

Joe: I've got it all at home.

Phil: I would have been there and done those people in.

Joe: I believe you would have. Bruce Halstead gave me that out of his own library. He signed his name.

Phil: He signed it. This is great. This is from a private library. Let's see what the date is on it. Private library 1991, that's over ten years ago. I knew it had been out for quite some time.

Joe: He incorporated paramagnetics in some of the things he was doing in the last part. He believed that by using DMSO, paramagnetics and camphor, you could stimulate the immune system from the outside of the skin to the inside. You didn't have to inject anything.

Phil: You didn't have to inject it because the DMSO goes directly into your skin.

Joe: The last thing Halstead did was introduce oxygen to DMSO to oxygenate it. When he oxygenated it, it took the taste away and it didn't have that crappy taste. They changed it to MSM.

Phil: I can take this paramagnetic dirt and put it in something that tastes real lousy and it would come out tasting good. It always switches it from a bad taste to a good one.

Joe: I can take water and put it inside the hyperbaric chamber, bring it up to three atmospheres and leave it there overnight. When you cap the water and take it out, it is living water.

Phil: The ancients knew a lot about this as a healing thing. All the old stone circles and stone structures, I need to write a book about them because I have photographs of them. I have copies of these stone structures. They are all around.

Joe: When you put a person in the hyperbaric chamber, it is an iron chamber, you are getting the orgone effect too. You can take the magnetic iron oxide crystal, lay it in the sun, a pad of them, and put them inside the chamber with you, with quartz crystals in those and let the sun charge them. I found out when you take them out of there, you always have to put them under an ultraviolet light to get off any sweat or anything that's coming off of the person. It could smell real bad because you sweat. You put them back in the chamber with them and raise it up and let them breathe pure oxygen. Man, you've got them going.

Phil: It makes them smell sweet again.

Joe: What do you think about putting people on a teaspoon full of magnetite or a few capsules of magnetite before you put them in the chamber?

Phil: I think that would probably triple or quadruple the effect of the chamber. Paramagnetism amplifies whatever is good and kills whatever is bad. Whatever poisons are in your body, it does away with and whatever is good, it enhances. It enhances all the vitamins in the body. But if you have some arsenic from the soil or something that's not too good for you, it gets rid of it. If you go back and read the old literature, you begin to understand that Easter Island, where the big statures are.. those are healing statues. The body is a natural antenna. The statue is a natural antenna. You can put a small amplifier on it and pick up a radio signal a lot better than you can with a metal antenna. The statue is like a natural antenna.

Joe: That doctor from Japan, Higgins' friend, has found the structured water. Your mind can structure to water. Dr. Tori told me that your mind has to be present and you have to have the right thoughts in order to structure the water. There is a doctor in France at the Pasteur Institute whose name was Jacques Benefiste. He wrote a book on water called "The Memory of Water".

Phil: I've heard of the book.

Joe: I spent ten days with him in Hawaii where we talked about this for a long time. It got to where he can speak pretty good English. We got along really well. He was telling me that when you magnetize the water, the water can take on its memories. But, if you distill the water and it is completely dead, then you don't have the living properties of the water.

Phil: That's right. If you distil it, there is nothing in it. It's just pure H2O and it is not what nature had in mind. Water is filled with minerals and vitamins and many other things. If a butterfly wants to live a long time, it stops at a muddy puddle and takes a drink. You'll always find butterflies all around the country where it's drying out and there are mud puddles.. filled with butterflies.

Joe: But you won't find them drinking the water that's in a stream.

Phil: No, they won't drink the stream water at all. They will always drink from the mud puddles. They won't go near a clear stream.

Joe: Like the people in India, the pregnant women that take these little mud balls.

Phil: Well, not so long ago, my mother who died at 89 was really quite healthy. During her pregnancy, she would go dig some clay out of the garden and eat it. She was part Indian. That's why we are shaped the way we are. My ancestors founded New Mexico. (San Juan) He was the first governor of New Mexico.

Joe: A few years back we did the whole de Anza Trail.

Phil: This was my great great great grandfather. Everybody said well he wasn't even married. Well, of course not.. he had a couple of Indian squaws and didn't bother getting married. He was quite a character. He was a Colonel in the Spanish army that came over to Mexico City, came north up the de Anza Trail to settle in Santa Fe. He's my great great great grandfather.

Joe: Those pressurized balls. I call them the Langévin balls because Paul Langévin is the one that actually showed you how. If you want to put them under pressure, you just dry them. I use pascalite clay as the binder. I place a drop of sodium silicate on a disk that's laying on an angle.. going around and around. That's why they're different sizes. Then I drop the magnetite and I have been sonically grinding sapphites that I got from India. I get them at the rock show in Tucson. I grind them up and mix them in it. That makes them very hard. If you take a ball like that and rake it across glass, it will score it just like a diamond.

Phil: I take paramagnetic rock and mix it with Elmer's glue to bind it.

The glue is diamagnetic and the rock is paramagnetic, so you have the perfect medium.

Joe: Elmer's glue is a hoof glue isn't it?

Phil: Yeah, Elmer's glue is made out of hooves. It's made out of horses hooves. They used to use horses for dog food and the hooves for glue.

Joe: So you get the yin and the yang.

Phil: You have got the yin and the yang. Elmer's glue is one of the best things to make anything. You can mix paramagnetic rock with Elmer's glue and make statues.

Joe: If you took magnetite, a little bit of quartz and Elmer's glue, and painted over a house, you would actually have a Faraday cage, wouldn't you?

Phil: Yeah, that's actually what this is. (**Phil scratches the wall**). It's slightly paramagnetic. So this house is a real energetic house. It's very relaxing.

Joe: It's a Faraday cage. This is something I didn't tell you. The old Spaniards when they were making the adobes, they killed animals and what they'd do is lure them in with salt licks. When they killed the animals, they would take the blood out and mix it in the adobes. Now, you have a paramagnetic adobe block.

Phil: There's all of the round towers in Ireland. If you go back and read about the monks in ancient Latin, they always mixed the cement with oxen blood. They would take six or seven oxen to build a round tower and slaughter them to put it all into the mortar. Those towers are sitting on the ground with no foundation or anything and have been standing there for fifteen hundred years. There are still forty of them left. Most of them have been struck by lightening. There were originally about a hundred and fifty of them. Forty remain in perfect condition. They have been sitting on the ground with no foundation or anything for that long.

Joe: It's almost antigravity, isn't it?

Phil: Antigravity. It is. The force of the paramagnetism in the oxygen reacts with the force of the paramagnetism in the earth.

Joe: So, in earthquake country, if you poured your foundation with magnetite in it, it would never fall.

Phil: It would never fall. There are tower houses in Japan and also in Ireland and England which would be damaged in earthquakes. But the tower houses never fall down.

Joe: What if they took these piers and the bridges and put a shell around the outside of them using magnetite impregnated cement?

Phil: It would make it a lot stronger. It would stand up a lot better in an earthquake. That's what they should do in San Francisco.

Joe: I was looking for gold in Brazil and ran into Bruce Halstead who was there looking for green medicine. You, however, were down there just for the pure science aspect.

Phil: Yeah, I was just down there learning about the headhunters. I already knew a little bit about them, but I learned a lot more about them. They were well aware of paramagnetism. They had a magic word for it. They knew all about it.

Joe: Some of those women down there knew all about poisons.

Phil: Oh Go, yeah. They had drugs down there. They could take drugs out of a plant and you wouldn't know what it was.

Joe: Have you ever noticed how the men treat their women when they all know of about those poisons?

Phil: Yeah.

Joe: They treat them real nice. No one is beating anyone.

Phil: They have great respect for their women. There is none of this tribal stuff that goes on as with some tribes where women are second rate. With the headhunters, the women are equal with the men. The men consider them their equals. The ones I knew were called the Ashiari and they were remarkable. I guess I was the first one to ever come across them. I came across them at the Hagramona River which means River of the Tapers. I got in the canoe. My wife never worries about me, but everyone else was telling her, "He's not going to come back. He's not going to come back." She just laughed. She thought it was funny. She knew darn well I was coming back because the headhunters were the friendliest people. In fact, they were over friendly. They couldn't do enough for you. They were so friendly it was nauseating. They were always around you doing something for you.

Joe: I told his wife one time about you that you're a very even tempered person. I've never seen you get mad. She said, "Just make your card out. Just mention Monsanto to him."

Phil: Yeah, they have probably done more to destroy people in this country than anyone else. They're a big corporation.

Joe: What do you think about these new genes that they're trying to make calling them "terminator seeds"?

Phil: All that research is just funded by the devil is what it is. There is a devil, and it is funded by the devil. It's evil spirits in Indian literature.

Joe: You took a picture one time of a little old man or woman praying in the church with the light rays coming through the window that bent. I never could understand what bent.

Phil: Well, the light coming through travels in a straight line, but it's traveling through oxygen. When people get into a meditative state, they become so highly paramagnetic it pulls the oxygen down. The only way you can see light is if it has particles in it. So light has to have particles of dust, which means the light beam carries paramagnetic properties. You cannot see a laser beam if there is no dust or smoke in the air. So the dust or smoke, or whatever it is, is paramagnetic. So, when someone starts praying, it kind of bends it down. There is a scientific explanation for all of this stuff. What the ancients called "magic" is a science.

Joe: What do you think about all these paintings of the saints depicted with auras around their bodies? Do you think that is paramagnetic?

Phil: Yeah, sure it is. They are so close to God, that their brains actually give off photon coherent light. Because it is coherent, it is real bright. You'll notice that although it is painted as yellow in pictures, it is never really yellow, it is white. It is perfectly white as white as this wall. It is pure rays of white light.

Joe: This lady that was in India, Mother Theresa, she came to Phoenix and I went up and looked at her. I don't know if it was just me, or the way the light was, but it looked like she had a radiance around her.

Phil: Yeah, I met her assistant and the assistant had the same sort of radiance around her. She had a blue and white gown on.

Joe: The Dahli Lama comes to Tucson every once in a while. He has a field and two or three of the people around him that are real close have it.

Phil: Where is he living?

Joe: Well, he stays in California a lot. He has a colony in Tucson at Catalina and they come through. He was very close to a fellow that did a lot of research on Reis monkeys and imported all the Reis monkeys during the test. His name was Tom Slick. Have you ever heard of Tom Slick? He owned the Flying Tigers and the Young General (inaudible). He was killed in a plane crash. But he was working on this paramagnetic iron with me for a while. While he was alive, I got a thousand dollars a month every month to experiment to teach with it. We got very close.

Phil: He was quite a guy. I didn't realize he was killed.

Joe: He was killed in a plane crash just outside of Phoenix. The thing I handed you there, on the last part was a little bit about us when he was working in Tucson.

Phil: He was a stunt flyer.

Joe: He did a little of everything. He was a wealthy old man on his own. He would have a big circus tent down in Dallas and he would invite all kinds of nutty people. They would come in and he would have his secretary go around and take notes on what they were talking about. There were some real nuts. There were some guys who were going to build boats made out of ice. They were really way out.

Phil: They had a big party and everybody was drinking and there were all kinds of good food.

Joe: He was sort of a lesser well known "Howard Hughes". You've got a couple of hummingbirds that went right by the window.

Phil: Yeah, we have a feeder out there. They head for it.

Joe: Halstead was into birds. When he died, he had probably fifty different birds, big birds in cages from all over including South America. The kids divided them all up and took them to other places. They made a lot of noise and I don't know if any of them survived. I think there were a few in the cage at the Center. He never got into computerization. He did all his work by longhand and typed things out.

Phil: That's like me. I've never used a computer.

Joe: He has hundreds of thousands of things on record that he has done in his lifetime. Every time I go over there, I take $400 or $500 and they let me take anything out that I want and copy it. I've copied everything on HBO [hyperbaric oxygen]. I've copied almost everything they had on cancer. I've copied all of Royal Rife's stuff. I've copied all of Gersten's stuff. I've copied everything he had on the files. When I die, they're going to have a party or a yard sale. None of my kids are interested in any of that. I can't get any of them interested in it. They go to college, they get an education, and they're school teachers. And you know something Doctor, they will make of flip doing that. But the teachers aren't teachers anymore.

Phil: That's not true. My son is fascinated by this stuff. One of my daughter's is too. She teaches English in Mexico City. She's fascinated by it.

Joe: What's happening to the general public is what I'm talking about. I'm talking about everybody, my own kids.

Phil: I don't know. It's TV. They put the same thing on. I sit there and watch TV and after about 10 minutes, I get up and come in here and start reading because it's the same thing over and over and over. It's all violence. There's so much violence in this country.. that's called imprinting. They are imprinting people with all of this.

Joe: I think anyone who has ever read the complete works of O'Henry has seen every damn TV program that has ever been on.

Phil: Yeah, there was no plot that he didn't plot. If you read O'Henry, you've got all of them. But on TV it's the same thing over and over again. It gets boring watching it after a while. CSI is not too bad because it's a good detective story. They ought to go back to Sherlock Holmes.

Joe: And yet, he was on drugs.

Phil: Yeah, he was on drugs. He was a cocaine addict. Sherlock Holmes was the character, and O'Connell actually wrote it. O'Connell was a drug addict, so of course he had to put Sherlock Holmes on drugs too.

Joe: I don't think drugs are as bad as tobacco. I think tobacco is the worst thing in the world.

Phil: I agree with you. It killed my father. He was a chain smoker. He was an old cowboy and would roll his own. He came from Terre Haute, Indiana, but he spent most of his life in Texas and New Mexico. He was a car salesman and all of his customers were cowboys. He was a cowboy himself. He was a great rider. He had a horse called "Big Red" that could jump a ten foot fence. He was in the army cavalry. He died in 1963 from smoking. He kept smoking cigarettes all his life. He rolled his own and smoked them and finally got heart trouble then died.

Joe: Well, I think tobacco is one of the worst things there is. It kills four hundred thousand a year at least.

Phil: Oh yeah, at least it's gone way down because the young people don't smoke like they used to. When I was growing up, everybody smoked except for me.

Joe: I went to Salem, South Carolina and went to a factory there to see how they were making tobacco. They don't do it the way they used to. They take the whole stalk, the stem and everything and they throw it in a shaker and shake the stuff off of it and grind it all up. Then they run it like newspaper through rollers. They save the juice that's squeezed out, take shredded newspaper and add the juice back to it at the levels needed. They have stuff in barrels from Turkey that is also added. They call it deer tongue. Then they spray it with petroleum so it won't go off. Then they flavor it with brown sugar to make it sweet. These people don't even know what they're getting.

Phil: No, they're getting a big mixture of poisons.

Joe: Every bug in the world avoids tobacco. But, when a commercial poison doesn't work, they just add another one and another one and another one. They have four or five poisons on them.

Phil: Sure, it's a conglomeration of fifty or sixty poisons.

Joe: And all these bugs can build up an immunity to this stuff.

Phil: It's really bad to inhale cigarettes. Cigars are not so bad because they're pretty natural. They just take the tobacco and roll it up. But even that is not right anymore because now they spray the tobacco with chemicals. The FDA said they had to quit spraying tobacco because the insecticides are ruining the biological controls. The insecticide business has been done in by people like me. It's all biologically controlled now.

Joe: What about mad cow? Do you think it's just a mineral deficiency?

Phil: It's parathian poisoning. The cure for the warble fly was to take parathian and rub it into the wound. Think how stupid that is. Parathian is a censroide, which means your nervous system goes kaput. Censroide is the chemical that keeps your nerve endings working. So if you foul up your censroides, you become a nervous wreck. Someday they'll learn about Parkinson's disease with these people. It's probably from messed up censestorids from smoking.

Joe: I'll get you some paperwork. I met Dr. Joel Wallach. He wrote "Dead Doctors Don't Lie". He was a veterinarian who said, "If I treated people the way the doctors taught me to treat them, as a medical doctor, I would be out of business. If you couldn't treat arthritis and you couldn't treat Alzheimer's in a cow, the cow is unable to access medicinal food. I do real good with the animals that I treat." He's done a paper on Alzheimer's and he's getting me a copy. I'm getting to be slow on memory.

Phil: Sure, I am too.

Joe: Sometimes I'll get out driving and go right past the place where I'm supposed to go. And I'm thinking about something else.

Phil: You're thinking about something something else is why.

Joe: But I am getting slower. I had a heart problem and they put two stints I me. They cut me open and put them in. The doctor said I had a heart that was young as hell, but it was just blocked off. And that's the way I'm eating. But I think if I had enough paramagnetics in me, I don't think I would have ever had heart trouble.

Phil: That's right. What I think you need to do if you have heart trouble is to start taking a teaspoon of paramagnetic dust every day and that would get rid of it. Put it in your orange juice.

Joe: Should it be really finely ground magnetite, or should it be just coarse stuff?

Phil: It's better coarse really, because it's more like an antenna. But it doesn't make that much difference. On the CGS meter it might be a difference of one CGS or something like that, but not enough to make that much difference.

Joe: Well I've got that 19,000 stuff. I don't think it will hurt me.

Phil: No, no. It would cure your heart trouble. Put it in your orange juice. It goes good in orange juice.

Joe: I don't know if I told you about this, but I made some solar stills for distilling water. I put magnetic iron oxide in the bottom of the stills. After a year or two the calcium will form on the iron. You take it out, pour little vinegar over it, clean it up then put it right back in. With these little tiny points sticking up in the air and when the sun shines in on the water, the vapor seems to break up and you can get twice as much water.

Phil: Sure, You have an ultrasonic condition taking place. When I start running the water, the birds nearby start talking and singing because the ultrasonics comes from the water. Parrot owners don't know that. Some parrots will talk once in a while just to imitate sounds, but you can get a parrot to talk a blue streak by putting some ultrasonics near it. Birds hear by ultrasonics.

Joe: Now, if you take a disk with lots of quartz and a little electricity and put it in water, the water will broadcast it throughout the room.

Phil: When you turn a faucet on, it's ultrasonically dynamic because the water runs past a metal faucet which creates a lot of ultrasonics. If you take the bird in the bathroom and turn the faucet on, it will start talking.

Joe: If you take the water and iron oxide tape, like an audio videotape and you record the water, you have the frequencies. If you play that for the bird, it would do the same thing, wouldn't it?

Phil: Yep, it would make the bird sing all day long.

Joe: I have a whole set of tuning forks. I record each of the tuning forks. I can take the tuning fork and make it work with another fork over here. I can make a tape of that tuning fork and play it turned up and amplified and it will do the same thing because it's the same frequency. And that's what scares me. Benefiste said he can replicate the same frequency of opium from Los Angeles and broadcast it over the telephone and make a guy go higher than a kite in New York.

Phil: Sure, everything is a frequency. That's all it is. You can record anything you want and make it do good, or make it do bad. People were tortured just by having a drop of water hit a certain surface which creates a certain sonic sound that would drive people crazy. They have been tortured with a drop of water creating an ultrasonic frequency just by hitting the right surface.

Joe: Well, I think the understatement of the year was, "The author firmly believes that this work is his most important and he can save agriculture worldwide. By Dr. Phil Callahan." I think that says it all.

Phil: Yep, yep. Well a lot of people are still buying that book.

Joe: I buy them by the case. Once in a while, the ones you have autographed for me get away. This one hasn't even been signed. You can sign it for me.

Phil: I can sign it right now.

Joe: I try to keep them at home. I buy them by the case from you. I put them out all over. I have a half dozen at these at the Biosphere where they were working up there. A couple of Chinese Ph.D.s were working up there and they took this book back to China with them. That's why they are ordering paramagnetics from me. They are starting a place in Loma, China, which is very similar to Arizona. They are putting a big glass dome over in China. You've signed almost all my books. I've got every book you ever put out. Thank you. You've got some books you haven't published.

Phil: I've got a whole stack of books around here somewhere.

Joe: Oh, I have to share with you another thing. Dr. Halstead, during the last part of his life, wrote a book on coral calcium. A whole book. He sent it to me and I read the transcript then wrote back to him. By then it had gone to print. I said that if you take the coral calcium and blow it apart with sound instead of pulverizing it the mineral will be cellularly assimilated. It wouldn't hurt to add a little lignites and iron oxide. He followed through with the suggestion and reported that the growth on the stuff, as well as the animals that he fed it to, were unbelievable. The stuff assimilated. It didn't pass right through the system.

Phil: The funny thing is when you tell that to a veterinarian, they go right home and use it. When you tell that to an M.D., they look at you like you're crazy. The vet will go right home and go to work on it.

Joe: So, most of these medicines that we're making are beaten, hammered, ground and compounded. The vitamins and minerals are ruined. It's so easy to blow them apart. Tesla was the one that started using sound to blow apart minerals. Tesla almost collapsed an entire building down with a police whistle.. sound!

Phil: Tesla and Wilhelm Reich were the two geniuses with this sort of thing. They didn't know the physics of it, but they knew what they were doing.

Joe: I did not get to meet Tesla. I went up there when I was a young kid, and he didn't like kids. I was trying and he didn't want anything to do with me. But Wilhelm Reich came to Tucson and lived with me for 18 months during the last part of his life. His son was my age and we got along really well. He wrote a couple of things. You'll read a little in that paper about Wilhelm Reich.

Phil: Wilhelm Reich was a psychiatrist and he loved children. Tesla was a loner.

Joe: In fact, any money Wilhelm Reich made was supposed to go in a children's protection fund. Now, he's been dead fifty years as of this year. He said the last part of his research would not be able to be made public until the fiftieth year. So, I'm going to go back to Rainley, Maine where there's a lady that's in charge of the center. I'll copy everything that I can get. I usually drag Marilyn around with me to see that I get where I am going. God, she's put up with me for fifty years. People around Tucson call her Saint Marilyn.

Phil: Well, my wife's put up with me for fifty-four years. Like everybody said, she married a character.

Joe: You met your wife in England?

Phil: Ireland.

Joe: You learned so much in Ireland about the salt and paramagnetics.

Phil: I learned a lot of from the old stone structures. I used to spend my time going around painting pictures.

Joe: You and Christopher Bird had the same kind of exposure in England. He was running the tower stations trying to redirect the airplanes and he was putting those things out.

Phil: I did the same thing actually. I was a Navigational Aides Expert and so was he.

Joe: He told me one time that they sent him to Germany to do some espionage over there. He went to France. Somebody was going to send in a bunch of plastic explosives. They made a mold in the form of lobsters.

Some idiot had the idea to make them red. As they unloaded the lobsters off the boat, the Germans realizing the peculiarity of tossing out cooked lobsters ended up killing everybody on the boat. A lobster doesn't turn red until you cook it.

Phil: You have to cook it to turn red. They knew something was wrong.

Joe: So, the Germans killed everybody there. He said he just barely got out alive. Whenever I got to talk to Christopher Bird, he was always interested in what you were doing. A lot of times I didn't know what you were doing because you didn't talk much about anything.

Phil: Well, I never talked much about World War II until I would get the Medal of Honor. I was an unofficial spy. I sent data back to the OSS before it was the CIA and the German's occupied France. (**points to a picture**) In fact, that's one of these airplanes. A B-26.

Joe: Do you do your own artwork?

Phil: Oh yeah, this is mine.

Joe: That's beautiful.

Phil: This is all mine. I just finished these for the book. That's a ship that went down.

Joe: Art Brown did a lot of his work too.

Phil: This is a hen harrier. It depends on if you want to kill birds, rats or mice. That was the best falcon I ever had. I would hunt rats and mice with him because what would I want to kill a bird for? The hen harrier is a large bird. I would go around a farm and kick the haystacks so rats would come out.. the falcon would get them. We call it a marshal in this country. They call it a hen harrier over there... same bird found all over the world.

Joe: Roy Davis told me about the birds in the Everglades getting iron oxide in their brains for sensing direction. He studied that for a long time and he found out that the gray Spanish moss growing on the trees have an affinity for iron oxide. The moss takes it into the plants. The birds would eat the berries off the Spanish moss and that's how they get the magnetite into their system.

Phil: That's exactly true, because I've seen them eating those berries. They're getting all the good stuff from the Spanish moss that goes into those berries. I'm going to publish a book that's mostly paintings.

Joe: Halstead worked closely with fish and the ocean. He put some huge books together because he had an oceanography degree, but he was still interested in birds. There's not a lot of difference between birds and fish.

Phil: Birds are actually reptiles. That's why they have scales on their legs.

Joe: Did you ever see any of Gould's books out of England? The books are worth a fortune now.

Phil: Come here, I'll show you something.

Joe: Gould taught me a lot about looking for minerals.

Phil: Did you ever meet him?

Joe: No, never met him. I met people that met him. Those books are selling for thousands now, did you know that? Gould wrote about how birds can lead you to minerals. The Gould stuff is selling for a fortune.

Marilyn: Let Dr. Callahan talk a little bit too.

Joe: Go ahead. I want you to talk.

Marilyn: He does those? Those were beautiful.

Phil: This is a hen harrier, which is a bird of Ireland.

Marilyn: That's right, I remember reading in your book that you like birds.

Phil: I'm getting a Medal of Honor, so I figured I better write a book. This is my old B-26 that I flew. I was a radio gunner, but I flew it too.

Joe: He's a hell of an artist, isn't he?

Marilyn: That bird is beautiful.

Joe: Marilyn, why don't you sit down here and direct a little bit and get him to talk about himself.

Marilyn: You had things you were going to ask him. Are you running out of stuff?

Phil: A lot of what you see around here is stuff I've done. That's an old German legend. That cross there is (inaudible) and that's a redheaded woodpecker which is common in Louisiana. It's not too common around here, although I've seen one or two. That's my golden eagle I trained as I would a falcon.

Joe: You actually were able to train it?

Phil: Oh yeah, I found the eagle. I had it for about 10 years. Finally, I had to move temporarily and I couldn't keep the eagle in an apartment. So, I donated it to the New Orleans Zoo. It must be forty years old now. It's in the New Orleans zoo and still alive. They live to be 50 or 60 years old, but that eagle is still alive in the zoo. At least he was a year ago. (**points**) Those are in my paintings there. The painting of the Indian is not mine. That was painted by Yazu. He was one of the great Indian painters.

Joe: Birds have a close relationship to man, more than we realize. The canaries were used in the mines to warn the men when there were dangerous levels of carbon monoxide.

Phil: They always took with them a canary. If they got too much methane, and the canary would keel over, they would take the canary and leave.

Joe: What do you think about these new bio-toxins that Halstead was developing? Do you think that it would be better to use birds to check them rather than men?

Phil: Nothing can poison a bird or a snake. I used to have a little grass snake, a cave snake, about that long. It looks a little bit like a rattlesnake. They don't lay eggs like most snakes, but give birth to live snakes. It was really funny because they got out of their cage once and all these little ones got out.

Joe: Did you experiment with snakes on bio-toxins?

Phil: Yeah, and I did infrared experimentation with them. Their tongues could detect the heat.

Joe: Can a snake and a bird detect poisoned water and food?

Phil: Oh yeah, you can't poison a bird. If there are no birds around the water, you know it's no good.

Joe: You could pour that water over iron oxide and it would be free of poison.

Phil: Yeah, that's what I did in World War II. When I wanted a drink of water, and I would have a rock in my pocket and I would throw it into the canteen and drink it. I never got sick. You just throw a bunch of paramagnetic rocks in the canteen. I could take rocks out of any old ditch, put it in polluted water and have water. I was a radio commando and I had to have water. You can live a week without food, but you have to have water.

Joe: So you dropped your paramagnetics into your canteen and you had water. Now why don't they put a couple of these paramagnetic balls in the water canteens for every soldier?

Phil: Sure. That's why, in some ways, God has taken care of things. On Memorial Day, I'm going to be on TV. I'm going to be in Washington with the President and getting my Medal of Honor. So, I'm going to tell everyone about paramagnetism. Then it will catch on like wildfire because someone with a Medal of Honor will be up there telling them about it and they will believe. The doctors will even start to believe.

Joe: Paramagnetics is God's gift to man. Why don't you tell about the statues you drilled holes in the bottom and filled with paramagnetics? (To Marilyn) He carries it in his pocket all the time. I've never seen him when he hasn't got it in his pocket.

Phil: I've had this in my pocket ever since the Army. It's filled with paramagnetic rock. It's a novel statue and it's filled with paramagnetic rock. I never catch a cold or get sick or anything.

Joe: Notice the parallels between Dr. Callahan and Dr. Vogel. They were both very religious. In that one article I gave you today, he put the paramagnetic iron, the magnetite iron in oil. He sat down and he looked at it and looked at it and he kept thinking about the Virgin Mary and it formed in the oil. It's in that article. It's unbelievable.

Marilyn: You remember that guy that used to come to Tucson? I believe his name was Richard. He put magnetite in ballpoint pen cases and carry them.

Phil: Yeah, I remember that. Vogel and Reich did the same thing too.

Joe: I still have a Wilhelm Reich box in Tucson.

Marilyn: Oh, you do?

Phil: I've built one and it works real good.

Joe: He used rusty iron oxide coming off of steel wool and stuff like that. I found you're a lot better off to go to the pure oxide from the iron and take the magnetic iron oxide from magnetite, or black paramagnetic sand.

Phil: When I was in Ireland, I would take a rusty tin can, scrape all the rusty iron oxide off the tin can. About the same time, Elmer's glue came out during the war. I would mix it with the pure iron oxide. I had a little peanut tube and I would use a big square of that and power my own radio. I would carry it behind the hedgerows to make sure no one was following me.

Joe: He told me that Elmer's glue, which is the hoof of a horse and is diamagnetic, and iron oxide which is paramagnetic, and mix them together, you have the perfect deal.

Phil: You've got the perfect yin and yang. The Chinese knew all about yin and yang. They knew that plants were diamagnetic and rocks were paramagnetic.

Joe: Well, five thousand years ago, they were using paramagnetics for their compasses.

Phil: The first compass used had paramagnetic rock. They actually floated. It would float even though it was rock, it was in diamagnetic water and the paramagnetic property of it repelled to keep it up.

Joe: Well, I don't know. He's learned so much. He's talked about the pads that he made to wear out of magnetic iron oxide, clay and salt water. Why was the salt water from sea salt so important?

Phil: Because it has every natural element that you need for your body. In other waters, salt water is the same as your blood. Salt water is just blood without hemoglobin. That's why they can substitute saline solution for blood sometimes.

Joe: I've got another one to share with you that's really unbelievable. I've taken seaweed, compressed it. Used it for a filter and I can get stuff out of water that doesn't even assay. This filter will take out minerals, ionics, and colloidals. It will take them all. All you have to do is wash the stuff and clean it up and you can use it over and over again.

Phil: That's all they used on the coast of Ireland. It's almost impossible now because of the chemical companies, but in the old days, that's all they used. They would collect the seaweed left up on the shore which is what this little vial is. It's carrying turp and it's carrying seaweed too. That's turp which they cut in the bog and burned for the bark.

Joe: That turp that they burn is mosslike and it is very close to being lignite.

Phil: That's why the old Irish islanders were so healthy. They were burning something close to lignite. It didn't have the sulfur and so didn't ruin your lungs.

Joe: Marilyn, he just said he mixes the iron oxide magnetite with Elmer's glue and paints it on the wall. It creates a faraday cage. It's a very healthy house, very healthy. There's no stray magnetic radiation.

Phil: That's an easy way to do it. Just plaster your walls with it.

Marilyn: He likes the möbius. He puts them all around.

Phil: Sure.

Joe: He's saying that the möbius is made with these plastics. And audio videotape records all this imagery on them and those are good, but he's saying that Elmer's glue is even better.

Phil: You can grind up rock and mix it with Elmer's glue then make just about anything you want. You can make a statue out of it or anything you want. I usually just buy a plastic statue and fill it with paramagnetic rock, but you could actually make a statue out of it. Other uses you can use it for would be to place it in the in every room of the house if you're under high voltage power lines. Spikes that occur with sixty cycle alternating currents are known as rougue electricity and it wreaks havoc with the body's electromagnetic balance. Magnetite around the house keeps the body in balance electro-magnetically.

Joe: Black Mountain, between Phoenix and Tucson, is primarily paramagnetic rock. Every winter it rains or sometimes snows. The mountain ices over and breaks it up. Then the sediment comes down as black sand. The further they go down, the finer they get. At the base of the mountain, paramagnetic rock has turned into pretty good sized crystals. Then about fifteen miles away they become very fine crystals.

Phil: I'll bet there is good plant life at the bottom of the mountain.

Joe: Oh, you can't believe the plant growth in there. Now, that's another thing I want to talk to you about. How does the magnetic iron oxide enhance the soil to the point that you can get by with less water?

Phil: Well, that's what happens around here with all this soil around here. Look how green everything is.. these trees. Everything is really green around here, and yet, we only get about twelve inches of rain a year. That twelve inches is like sixty inches in Florida because the paramagnetic soil holds the water. Instead of the water evaporating in two or three hours, the water evaporates in two, three or four days. If you have a puddle of water around here, it takes it days and days for it to evaporate.

Joe: The trees pick up this colloidal and ionic iron. Does that increase their ability to take the water through their cellular fiber?

Phil: Yeah. Those little tubules that go up the tree, the smallest one is called a microtubule. They bring the paramagnetic dirt up through them. You can't grow crops in sand like pure sand on a beach. You have to have paramagnetism in the soil. All good farm soil has to be paramagnetic. That's what has been destroyed with chemical farming. The more chemicals you put on, the more you have to put on.

Joe: I sold ten tons of iron one time to the Goeffe family, remember? They took it back to Intercourse, Pennsylvania. They were Mennonites. They had clay back there that had never grown anything. They took this magnetite from Arizona and spread it over the clay fields. They took clay that was worthless on its own and turned it into beautiful fields.

Phil: A lot of clay is paramagnetic. But just as much of it isn't. A lot of clay is just dead mud. When it rains, It's just dead mud. If you mix paramagnetic rock with it, you have diamagnetism of the clay and paramagnetism of the rock and you can grow anything in it. My original experiments were just with potted plants. I experimented with how much magnetism to use in each pot. I have notebooks on that.

Joe: Remember, we did the same thing with Dr. Ricketts. We put paramagnetics in one pot. The paramagnetic plants would be double the size of the other plants.

Marilyn: He did time released photos of them too.

Phil: Yeah, time lapse photography shows as a great demonstration of the growth.

Marilyn: Maybe we ought to do a video of that.

Joe: I love the old man, but he passed away. He was in his nineties and passed. I can't get along with the kid. The kid thinks only about money.

Phil: **(points)** That's one of the best books I have ever seen. It was written by an English soldier who was captured by the Germans.. he had a pet kestrel. The Germans really treated him good because they never saw a guy with a bird on his shoulder that would just sit there all the time. It's a great book.

Joe: You read a wide variety of books.

Phil: Yeah, I've got a little bit of everything up there.

Marilyn: Have you read "The da Vinci Code"? It's a new book out.

Joe: Marilyn got that the other day. I gave it to her to read.

Phil: Here is a picture of a paramagnetic tower house. They built a limestone castle on a tower house. It was very energetic. That's my wife's and my living room. That's where I asked her to marry me. Now it's been taken over by the tourist bureau, so it's a hotel now.

Marilyn: She told me you went on a world trip before you got married.

Phil: Yeah, I hiked around the world.

Joe: He had just his deep britches and his overshoes and a few matches in his pocket.

Phil: I had a 20 pound knapsack and a canteen. I carried a change of clothes and some granola bars.

Joe: The prickly pear cactus in Arizona form white matting on them from the cochineal bug. If you pull it off with a knife and rub it on a piece of white paper, it turns to a royal purple color. It's used as a dye. But if you reduce it down atomically, you'll find that royal purple contains gold. So, here's a plant that's extracting the gold from the soil that's showing up in the spun silk of the bug. The Spaniards knew that. They used to take this for dye and send it back to Spain. Then after they broke the coal down, they got all the colors of the rainbow out of the coal.

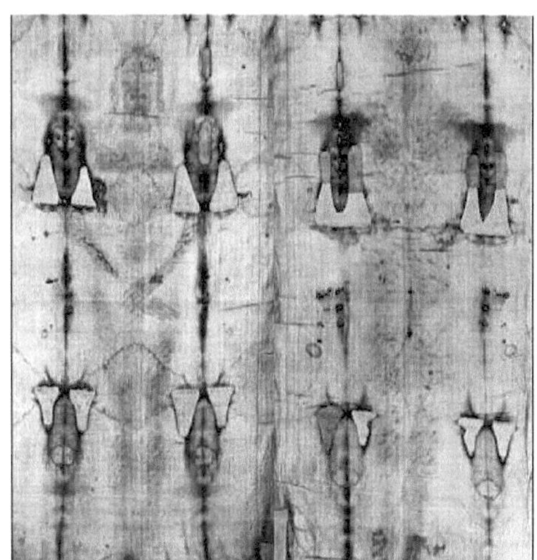

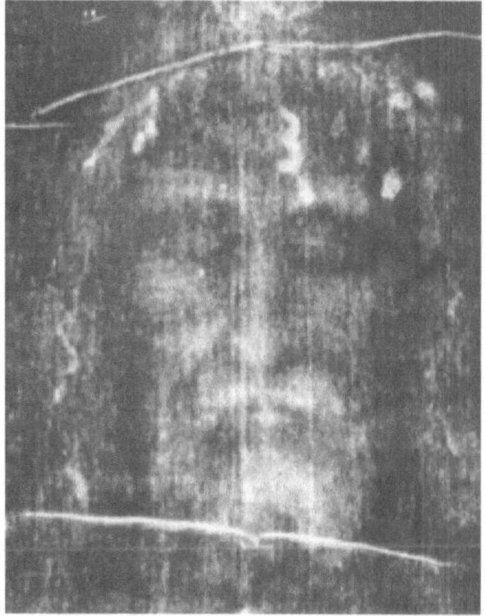

Marilyn: Now, what is this one here about Christ? I notice it is a Christ like picture.

Phil: That's the Shroud of Turin. That's the image that appeared on the shroud. I took that picture. I'm probably the only man that has touched the Tilma of the Virgin of Guadalupe, which is sacred in this country. On the Shroud of Turin, I was asked to come over and do an infrared study on both of them. I did an infrared study on the Virgin of Guadalupe.

Joe: Was that iron oxide on the Shroud of Turin, or was it red ochre?

Phil: It was iron oxide. Obviously, it came from the soil. What happened was when they laid the body on the shroud, the shroud was a long piece of cloth that folded over his body. On the bottom shows his back. It is on display now in Italy. It is behind glass so people can view it.

Joe: But it didn't come from the blood of the body, it came from the soil. Is that why people such as kings and queens in history have been buried in a river?

Phil: Some of it came from blood, like where it was really white. Apparently the water and blood were diamagnetic and repelled the paramagnetic. So, you have a lot of white spots, but the image itself was red ochre.

Joe: What about these people, these kings and queens in China, South America and even in Africa? They buried their royalty in red ochre.

Phil: Red ochre is considered a sacred soil. It is a sacred chemical too. It was used for healing as an ancient herbal.

Joe: But it doesn't have the healing aspects of magnetite, because magnetite is the end of the rusting process and ochre is going that way.

Phil: Ochre is going that way, but it doesn't make that much difference. You can take magnetite or rust from a metal tin can. Iron oxide is just more paramagnetic than red ochre.

Joe: You just get higher CGSs out of the end product.

Phil: Right. So, it slowly becomes highly paramagnetic.

Joe: Now, the blood itself is paramagnetic.

Phil: Blood itself is paramagnetic, but it's hard to measure because it's got so much water in it. If you use the CGS meter, it goes diamagnetic because you're measuring the water. It's like a transistor with trace elements of paramagnetism.

Joe: If you dehydrate the water and put the powdered blood plasma in...

Phil: Then it would be the other way which I have done by letting the water evaporate.

Joe: So you spent a lot of time on the shroud.

Phil: Oh yeah. I've got a paper on it somewhere.

Joe: I'd like to read that sometime.

Phil: I thought I had an extra copy around here somewhere. I don't even see one copy of it. I don't know what I did with it. That's a Security Service award. I got that for working on paramagnetism. The USDA believed me. I didn't have any problem with the USDA.

Joe: That's one of the first CGS meters?

Phil: No. It's an antenna. It's diamagnetic. That's a coil of string so I can see what I'm using for an antenna on the oscilloscope.

Joe: I bought a deal from Armand Bickell, the old man from Germany.

He did a lot of work for Von Braun and all the people in space. He designed that little thing to crawl around on Mars, an isotope discriminator. I bought one of his meter. I think your meters are more informative and I paid five thousand for that.

Phil: Yeah, those things are overpriced. It only takes about fifty to sixty dollars worth of electronics to put it together. Sosa makes a hundred dollar profit on it and sells it for four hundred and selling. The more people learn about paramagnetism the better the chance they buy them.

Joe: That fellow, Marshall, bought one. He came out and took one of those little film canisters, but then said, "I want all that my truck can haul. I want all I can take". You know, I used to give the stuff away. It got too expensive to give away, so I started selling it for a dollar a pound. They don't even say a word. When you sell ten tons at a dollar a pound, you've made yourself some money.

Phil: You've made a lot of money.

Joe: Pays the mortgage.

Phil: But if you're in the business, you have to.

Joe: But I've given it away for years and years.

Phil: Yeah, but you're getting older, so you need some money set aside so you can stay retired. You can't travel without money. You couldn't come here without money. It costs money to travel.

Joe: Damn sure of it. I've learned more from you than I have from Dr. Pye or all the people I've been really close to in all my life. They were geologists and engineers. They were educated in schools. But you have a kind of street knowledge. I call it real knowledge.

Phil: Street knowledge is what it is . Nature is my bride. I'm going to write a book and call it "Nature is my Bride". Nature has been my left hand besides my wife.

Joe: I met Schauberger. Hughes brought him over to Houston and I went down there to talk to him a while. He didn't speak English well. A lot of it got lost in translation. You and he are on the same frequencies. He was saying that fish can actually become paramagnetic and diamagnetic and they can actually levitate. They can go right up a stream. They can go right up a fall. He said they can be in a flow of water going downhill and go right up it.

Phil: Right, floating like a balloon up in the air.

Joe: He said the movement of the tail crates a vortex around the back of it and the water that is pushing them down is pushing them up. It's all magnetic. He said in the Rhine River at certain times with the full moon and paramagnetics, rocks on the bottom of the river will actually float. He had the idea that if you waited for the moon to be in the right position, and use the gravitational pull of the moon, you can float big hardwood logs out of a flume serpentined. It could not go in a straight flume, it would have to be broken up some way and serpentined.

Phil: That's the way the Hindus used to levitate. They would go into a paramagnetic room when the full moon was out. With the force of the moon and the paramagnetic room, they would levitate. Churches were paramagnetic actually. If you go back and read the literature about some of the people like Saint Bernadette, they actually levitated while in a paramagnetic church. Those gothic churches in old Ireland were all paramagnetic. They would go into a church made out of stone and get in a meditative state. They would become so highly diamagnetic, they would be totally relaxed. They become almost completely diamagnetic and the church just pulls them up.

Joe: When the paramagnetics in the stones get pressure on the top of them, there is a piezoelectric effect.

Phil: A piezoelectric effect, sure. You've got several different forces working. You've got the piezoelectric effect. You have the gravitational force being overcome by the force between the diamagnetism and the paramagnetism. When all these forces get together, you can actually levitate. That's how the ancient Indians used to levitate.

Joe: Vogel called that the fifth dimension.

Phil: That's what it is. It's another dimension when you can levitate. There are still some Indians who can do it. One place they used to do it was in the deserted villages out on the prairies of India, which were all paramagnetic. I have a picture of one around here somewhere. It is a mosque. A mosque was a great place for Indians to levitate.

Joe: The Hindus built their mosques with a round dome on the top and they established an antenna point

Phil: That's what this picture is. It's a round dome with an antenna. The vultures love to sit up there. All the vultures would congregate up there. The Black vulture had about a ten foot wing span. It would sit up on top of this mosque. All the lepers would congregate inside the Mosque. The Mosque was full of lepers. I went in there and slept for a couple of nights surrounded by lepers even though leprosy is very contagious.

Joe: Last time, you told me that leprosy was coming from the armadillo.

Phil: That was based on what I told one researcher. I said you ought to look on the pads of the armadillo feet, because armadillo get leprosy. He couldn't figure out why on the pad of their feet. leprosy is a soil bacteria that clings to their feet as they dig the soil.

Joe: Will leprosy grow in paramagnetic soil?

Phil: Oh yeah, that's a real mess. Leprosy is always at the bottom of that cliff. That cliff is all paramagnetic rock and it washed down to the shore where the leper colony was. The lepers were ostracized and put down there. Of course, the leprosy got worse and worse because they were down there where the soil was loaded with the bacteria.

Joe: So, the paramagnetics can cause the leprosy and the paramagnetics can cure the leprosy.

Phil: Paramagnetics enhanced the bacteria to the point where anyone that waked barefoot around there would get it. Leprosy is hard to catch until you sustain a cut anywhere the wound makes contact with the soil organism. The farmers in Hawaii will walk barefoot, but if they cut their foot and walk across that soil, they will catch it. It is a very slow condition.

Joe: You treated this stuff with paramagnetics.

Phil: Yeah, I treat it with paramagnetics. It's the same old thing. You treat the disease with the disease. It's a matter of concentrating it in the body and the immune system in the body. The diamagnetism in the body combined with the paramagnetism of the rock will cure leprosy. You can cure the disease with the disease you might say.

Joe: A frequency.

Phil: A frequency. Yeah. You have a frequency that is out of phase. You have the leprosy frequency and the paramagnetic frequency that is the same frequency, but it is a hundred eighty degrees out of phase, so they cancel.

Joe: Halstead said the reason we are having so much bad water is the fact that the hydrogen bond has changed its alignment.

Phil: It has changed its alignment completely. Probably also a lot of the paramagnetism in the water has been distorted by the water born poisons.

Joe: Won't running water over paramagnetic crystals realign it?

Phil: It realigns everything. It always gets rid of whatever is bad for life and enhances what is good. It always works that way.

Joe: Magnetic crystals are all sharp and they have dual polarity.

Phil: Right. They have antennas.

Joe: So, I look at it like if you are trying to clean water with marbles, you'll never get it clean. If you have sharp points, you clean it.

Phil: If you have sharp points, you clean it. Right. Which is why, if you take this paramagnetic grain, it's got billions of little antennas because you have so many little sharp points working to purify the water.

Joe: I talked to Ryner and two or three other people from Germany, and your book was the reason those people were treating the black forest with paramagnetics. They ground the stuff up and put it on the forest floor. Now why in the hell they do more of it in Germany if they know it works?

Phil: I don't know.. why don't they do it here? The farmers tell us to farm with it here. Leave it down the next day because it's so important. You tell it to the people and there isn't enough money involved in it. You buy paramagnetic block for twenty dollars a ton and put it on your farm instead of fife hundred a ton like fertilizer.

Joe: When you were at Acres last few times you were up there. I was out there last few times I was there waiting for you and you didn't show up.

Phil: Yeah, I'm going to go this year.

Joe: I'll make it this year.

Phil: I will, I'll make it this year.

Joe: Some of the Amish people wanted to talk to me about paramagnetics. They take you out to supper. What it means is a crock pot in a motel room, but it's good food.

Phil: Yeah, it's good food.

Joe: But anyway they were talking about this and were really disappointed that you didn't show up this last time. They're really nice and we talked a lot. Now, they have a bunch of your books.. These Amish people.. they have their own opinion.

Phil: I went to Acres twenty-five years in a row and I decided well.. but, ah, I need to go up there again because there's another generation coming along now talking about this generation.

Joe: The fellow that's running Acres is getting old too.

Phil: Yeah, well Fred is still young. Fred is in his fifties.

Joe: Last time I took him out to lunch he had a little trouble seeing. His eyes are going bad.

Phil: His eyes are going bad, yes. Chuck's eyes are really bad now and he's even my age. He's the same age as me about eighty-one. Fred's only fifty-three. He and his wife and so knock on wood. And so I'll probably go too.

Joe: I used to go to that Conference of Global Science in Denver. Yeah and they had some people up there to talk to. I should fly you over there one of these days to talk to the Breakfast Club.

Phil: I'm free most of the time. Just let me know when. You'll have to send a car over for me cause I don't drive anymore, well, if I can help it that is. I drive sometimes, but I let my wife do most of the driving

Joe: I drive sometimes but still don't know where I'm goin'.

Phil: Problem is, I haven't in years. My wife drives most of the time. I don't really like driving because it's just, well, the thing is I've done so much driving during World War II while I was in the military. That's why I walked around the world!

Joe: I let Marilyn drive all the way over here. I see over there you got a book on ants.

Phil: (**smiles, and turns to the book**) Yeah, I really like ants. That's a great book.

Joe: I used to go around the ant hills and pick up a magnifying glass and see what was under the ground. Ants bring bring your minerals up around the mound. You'll see the copper and silver.

Phil: Your mounds are coated with alabaster. You'll find that its coated with pink granite and quartz and ants go around and collect all the quartz and granite and line the whole hill.

Joe: Linda McCain used to put together a conference out in California on magnetics and various different things on all sciences. She'd invite people from all over the world to show up there. And, one time we went to her yard.. she put me up at her house. At a nice moment we had all these purty squirrels all over there and I took a five gallon bucket of iron and poured it one corner. Later, she called me back and says, "you know, all those little critters have moved to that corner where the paramagnetics is.

Phil: Oh, yeah

Joe: I gotta tell you a story over there. I went in with a truck and I had twenty-five gallon buckets weighing about a hundred pounds a piece. I went in to try to tell them the value of having magnetic iron oxide as a cold pack on the head or wherever you want it. A guy had a heart attack around the swimming pool. So, I went and got my little bucket and looked and saw that I had a little dry ice and a cold one and put one here and the cold one up against the back of his neck.

Phil: Yeah that'll do it. (**laughing**)

Joe: By the time the ambulance got there he was already stimulated and back to life. The guy says you ain't getting' any of these back, I don't know what they are but you ain't getting them back.

Phil: (**laughing**) You ain't getting them back, yeah...

Joe: So, everyone around there, everyone from the science committee were there and probably fifty people who said, "what was that?" I told them, "magnetic iron oxide". When they asked where they can get a little, I said, "I got a truck sittin' right out there in the parking lot" and I says, "There are ten or so buckets out there". Two hours later, there was not a single grain of sand left. They took every last one of them and the place had run out of little containers they were giving these people.

I didn't have anything to show.

Phil: They should have saved you some.

Joe: They had completely filled that place up with iron oxide. That made a lot of believers in your deal there. I told a lot of them and I said, "If you really want to know more about it get a hold of Callahan's book."

Phil: Yeah.

Joe: I printed your name and the title of your book on every piece of paper I handed out. I announced where to get it too.

Phil: It's been selling pretty good. According to Acres I think it'd be going on forever now.

Joe: I'd like to see you get that other one out there. How far off are you?

Phil: I got most of it. It's scattered around. I just got to put it together and jot stuff down here and there. I've got my autobiography, some about paramagnetism, my story written into it and how it works. Don't know what to name it yet. "Nature's My Bride," is what I was thinking.

Joe: It's a magic miracle.

Phil: It's the magic miracle. That's what it is.

Joe: Everyone knows what MMS is.. the magic miracle

Phil: Yep, the magic miracle is what it is.

Joe: Yeah, heh heh.

Phil: Well, the partnership picked it up. I don't know the medical profession is still in the chemical age, but ah, a doctor should have picked it up. Holistic doctors all over the country are using it.

Joe: There's a guy named Carter in Las Vegas has made a fortune. I just gave it to him. He made it into pads and he has these people come up to him and he soaks them in water and he adds deterium to the water, gold, and it's liquid gold... the liquid gold has a tendency to kill pain too. He puts MSM in with it so you don't have the taste of DMSO. He calls it "anti aging". Halstead said that all these minerals that I'd give you today are grown in paramagnetic soils. And they're herbs..

Phil: The herbs...

Joe: You've got to have good soil.

Phil: That's right

Joe: He said he'd have to go back into China. You have to travel far where they don't use the pesticides.

Phil: It's still good earth. In England and China they still have traditional farmers. The coast is mostly ruined, so, you go in a hundred miles where they still got good farmland.

Joe: Now, Halstead, just before he died.. they named two good herb gardens after him. They gave him a big gold piece of metal like that, a really nice piece of metal for his work on herbs.

Phil: On herbs.. that's right.

Joe: That was in the last book he wrote. The biggest improvement we made I think was on that coral calcium. You gotta be careful about that coral calcium. You can't get it where they've done that radioactive testing.

Phil: That's deadly

Joe: Remember when doctor.. you know, that doctor out in California at Scripts that was working with us on that. I did a paper on him up there. That Dr. Martin seeded the ocean with that black iron. We ground the iron down real fine and we mixed it with cotton seed oil and then air dried it using a fan so it would float on the ocean. He found that the algae would grow twenty-seven thousand times overnight and watch the whole ocean turn green...

Phil: Sure, sure, Yep, the ocean turns green.

Joe: …and the whole food chain started.

Phil: That's right.

Joe: But, Halstead come up with something. He said, "Joe, be careful about this because it feeds off other things and it goes out to the algae. It ruins the algae. When it gets to the algae it gets all over the coral. He said there's a little oceanic microbe called a titan. I'd never heard of it. But a titan has a series of teeth made out of magnetite, so they're magnetic, and they eat the algae. They'll eat the algae off the coral and then undermine the coral which falls over for lack of nutrients out of the bottom which is why it dies. He said this may be killing more of the coral than you realize. It's back to getting the iron. Be careful about trying to improve something that you don't have a bad side effect.

Phil: The coral is diamagnetic and you really don't want too much paramagnetism.

Joe: Well, Marilyn, why don't you talk to him some a bit about early life?

Marilyn: I've been talking to his wife about it, alot. I get it straight from the horses mouth.

Joe: Get him to talk about it a little bit. I asked Mrs. Einstein one time. I said, "You understand the Einstein Theory?" You know what she said, "no, better yet, I understand Einstein".

Phil: Yeah, right. (**turns to Marilyn**) You'll never guess where I was born.

Marilyn: Where?

Phil: Fort Benning, Georgia. In the officers club. What happened is is an interesting story.

Marilyn: In the officer's club, huh...

Phil: They moved my mother into the hospital when she was ready to deliver and that evening the hospital was sort of creaking. The more it creaked the more panicked the colonel that commanded the post got, so he moved right into that room there. My father come back and the twenty- fourth infantry was all black. And so they moved my mother out to the officer's club and that's where I was born. Not only was I born in the officer's club, I was born among the blacks. That hospital, well, it fell down the next morning. It collapsed.

Marilyn: Wow!

Phil: I got that from my sister. I remember that.

Marilyn: You can also say you brought down the house.

Phil: Yeah, I brought down the house. That's what my sister used to say and I'd ask, "what are you talking about", so she finally told me the story. My mother told her, but she never told me. My father who lived to sixty three knew and never told me. He smoked himself to death. My mother lived to be 89. She comes from a generation where the dead ancestors used to take quinine. So my mother would take it when she got pregnant. Actually the drugstores sold it to them.

Joe: It's still the main deal over in India. India still does it.

Phil: All the drug stores that make synicee sell quinine sell it sterilized.

Marilyn: You think she got her minerals that way?

Phil: It's the paramagnetics in it for the crazy deliveries.

Joe: Now wasn't the great epidemic, the influenza epidemic, started from burning common horse manure?

Phil: In the air.

Joe: A lot of airborne toxins. Got it in the air

Phil: Yep, got it in the air.

Joe: Became an airborne toxin.

Phil: An airborne toxin.

Phil: There's so few airborne toxins in the air around here because of the soil being so paramagnetic. You can't get sick around here even if you tried.

Joe: What do you think about these chemtrails that's running around about here? They're trying to keep the earth from warming up. You think they're taking micro magnetic iron and micro aluminum and dispersing it up in the air to stop it from warming?

Phil: It might work. It might slow down what's happening.

Joe: They're experimenting all over..

Phil: This industry is creating so much methane that it's destroying the atmosphere, actually. It gets clear up 300 miles into the atmosphere.

Joe: And if the ocean gets a little warmer the methane gets frozen down there at the bottom and it melts.

Phil: If it gets another degree warmer we'll get into real trouble. Scientists know that. There're laws in most states. I don't know about New Mexico, but I think New Mexico has a law too. They have to cut down on their methane emissions.

Joe: Well, we haven't talked much about politics. What do you think about our president?

Phil: Not too much.. he's not an ecologist. (**Joe begins to laugh**) Kerry cares about ecology. Bush is alright, but he ain't no ecologist that's the whole problem. He's an oil man.. that's the whole problem.

Joe: He appropriated millions of dollars for hydrogen, but he said he'd have to make it out of oil.

Phil: Yeah, that's the problem. It's money madness. I don't know whether Kerry is so money mad or not.

Joe: He married enough of it.

Phil: I think Kerry is probably alright. I think he's more of an ecologist than Bush. If Bush had learned something from his father.. I know both of them.. I know all three of them, but I don't know Kerry at all. I know Clinton very well. I went to school with him.

Joe: I didn't know that.

Phil: We went to school together and we taught together. I've had forty or fifty breakfasts with president Clinton I guess. But he was an ecologist too. Bush, he's totally oblivious to it and destroying the environment.

Joe: Clinton was smart. Clinton had a good mind.

Phil: Yeah, he was smart. He was a brilliant guy.

Joe: He had a pretty big ego.

Phil: Yeah, that's for sure. Damn straight on that, yeah.

Joe: That's how he'd get the best of them.

Phil: Yeah, I was the only one to put his ego down too. We went to school together and taught together. So, he knows me real well.

Joe: He gave us the largest surplus of money we ever had.

Phil: He did what the Republicans always come to do. What they did was drive us into debt. That's liberals.. whatever you want to call 'em. Clinton came along and that's the only time this country's ever been out of debt. He knew what he was doing. He's an economist.

Marilyn: I came here to see if you guys are getting a little hungry.

Joe: Take you to lunch?

Phil: Sure.

Joe: Okay.

Marilyn: But you know they're an hour ahead of us and my clock says one o'clock, but it's really two o'clock.

Joe: (**to Marilyn**) I'm going to talk to him tomorrow too. (**to Phil**) Your wife says you have good days and bad days. I'll stay when you have a good one.

Phil: I'll go to lunch with you all because I need a cup of coffee now.

Marilyn: Okay..

Joe: We had ribs last time we were here. Let's all go down to the rib house over here.

Phil: Yeah, that's right.. it's right here.

Joe: I could find the rib house but I couldn't find your house (laughs). Ask your wife to go with us.

Marilyn: She's getting dressed right now. She's getting ready to go.

Joe: Okay.

PART TWO

Marilyn: Did you paint one of these?

Phil: I painted the three over there on the wall, and these three here.

Joe: Unbelievable.

All three begin speaking at the same time

Marilyn: (**to the video camera**) Okay, these two were painted a year ago. Aaaaaand... Dr. Callahan painted these three.

Phil: My grandmother willed me those two pictures. She knew I wanted them. So when she died those were in her estate. I told her I had to have them and so I got them when she died. She was fairly wealthy.. inherited a lot of money from him.

Joe: The Spanish did a book on birds. They found that birds were animals that would eat certain seeds. The seeds would grow on certain environmental soil. (**video cuts out for a few seconds**)

Phil: Birds are.. they eat certain seeds.

Marilyn: (**to the camera**) The Spanish.. inherited..

Joe: That's how they found Ajo. Ajo means garlic in Spanish. That's how they found the copper.

Marilyn: And this is the view from the porch. Beautiful country. (**takes the video camera to show a panoramic view out the front door. The camera focuses on a sign above the door "Dad's Workshop" which is the garage behind the house**).

Phil: Everybody that goes there wants to go back.

Joe: How much time?

Phil: Because Ireland has a real good tourist bureau. The tourists really help you out.

Joe: After the dark ages, actually, was the depository of all the Catholic religion. Rome got so corrupt that...

Phil: ...Ireland and Scotland had all the ancient histories. There's a book about that called, "How Ireland Saved The World". They wanted to save the world.

Joe: Ireland did something with these big.. on top of these mountains..

Phil: Yeah, right.

Joe: ...they built water catchments and they put the clay underneath them. I'll bet that clay was paramagnetic.

Phil: It's paramagnetic, sure, they catch that water there for their farms. Yeah, they know how to irrigate.

Joe: They actually harvested.. they took it right out of the earth.

Phil: They knew how to irrigate the terrain. They did that experiment under them.. they catch that water. Yeah, they know how to irrigate.

Joe: They actually harvest.

Joe: I think maybe.. somehow or other we lost a lot of stuff in history of value.

Phil: They went to high technology and poisoned everything. Which.. it's changing now though. I got it changed pretty well. The Department of Agriculture is changing it completely. They've gone strictly towards organic farming now.

Joe: Anyone that's really done any studying with ecology.. you never really had the following that you should have had with this Greenpeace and all these other.. a lot of them were money. You never really had..

Phil: Greenpeace had enough money, and it started out good. They didn't have any use for it either.. they didn't even try.

Joe: It broke loose.

Phil: It broke loose, yes.

Joe: I haven't even talked to you about depleted uranium and all this perchlorate that's coming out of every military base. Perchlorate is scarin' the hell out of people.

Phil: It's poisons. It's what they're doing.

Joe: Every base in this country has just loaded the cities around them with perchlorates.

Phil: What do they say as to how these perchlorates work?

Joe: They believe it's coming out of the fuels.. the jet fuels.

Phil: Yeah, so it's coming out of the jet fuels..

Joe: ..and all this other stuff.

Phil: So it's poisoning the atmosphere.

Joe: Yeah, up in the air and their coming down. Maybe these chemtrails and all this other stuff.

Phil: They can clean that up, but they don't want to put any money into it. They don't mind puttin' it up there, but they won't pay to clean it up.

Joe: I think you can clean it up with these microbes. Like what Teruo Higa was doing with those effective microbes.

Phil: Real simple. It wouldn't cost much

Joe: Where these pig farms and chicken ranches and where all that stuff is. All that nitrogen is real good if you just worked it with a little carbon and you worked it with..

Phil: ..and then you'd clean it off.. It'd be real easy.

Joe: That's what I want to talk to you a little about and, (**to Marilyn**) "Are you ready?"

Marilyn: Uh hmmm.

Joe: Come over here and talk a little bit more and then when you get tired just holler and.. I'm not gonna wait another year to come over to talk. Next time I'm gonna see you before that.

Phil: Come over any time you want. The advantage of being retired is it doesn't make any difference when you come.

Joe: I thought I'd retire, but I just got tired (**Marilyn and Joe laugh**)

Marilyn: (**to Phil**) You can go in there and she can clean up in here.

Joe: You can come back and talk about anything you want.

Phil goes into the other room so that his wife can clean. The interview continues after he's rested.

CONTINUED:

Phil: Christopher Bird went there.. the reason he went there is because he is Jewish and he had to pray to the Virgin Mary. The day after he prayed to the Virgin Mary the Gestapo was after him. The Gestapo kind of opened up and he went through their lines. He went through the German lines without ever had been touched. He went clear across Germany. They never caught him.. they wanted him real bad because he was a very religious guy and he spoke out. He was a Jewish guy, but he was speaking out for the Catholic people to get up and fight Hitler. But he went right through their lines and when he got the words, he thanked the Virgin Mary for the words. He wrote a book.. a famous book about the words and it was written by a Jewish guy. It's called St. Bernadette of course. It sells copies every year.

Camera cuts off:

Phil: ... he could change electronics.. the world.

Joe: Well, HAARP and all these other things, that's his stuff.. it's not Eastmont's. It's Tesla.

Phil: Yeah, that's Tesla. He did it all. When you go back, you find out he started every bit of it.

Joe: Where'd he get his knowledge? How'd he get it? How'd he tune in?

Phil: Well, he used to say.. he'd say he was very spiritual and that it came from God. Same way I guess you'd say it was insight I guess is what you call it. He could just look at something and an idea would flash in front of his eyes.

Joe: Tesla believed that he could actually talk to E.T.s.

Phil: Sure.

Joe: He believed he could talk to people further than Mars.

Phil: There's no doubt he could. I don't doubt he was talking to people on Mars.

Joe: He said he was.

Phil: Well, If you re-photograph Mars with that fifty watt transmitter, that means by the time the energy reaches Mars which is a hundred and twenty-nine million miles away. So, if you got a fifty watt transmitter, by the time that energy gets back to the receiver, it's ten to the minus twenty-seven watts. You can't even say that. It's twenty-seven zeros. You can't even say that number. It's a trillion trillion trillion trillion trillion trillion trillion trillion of a trillionth of a trillionth of that little watt that you tune to. That's how sensitive our electronics is today. So, there's no problem at all photographing Mars or anything else. They're photographing other galaxies now by sending up satellites to photograph them.

Joe: Armond Bickell, he's still out at the Lompoc. He's about ninety years old now.

Phil: He's pretty old now.

Joe: I went to visit him a couple times and even bought a Bickell machine from him. I paid about five thousand dollars for that machine and I think your CGS machine does the same thing a bit better. It's a little easier to understand and you don't have to have a scientist and a PhD to run it.

Phil: Yeah, I know that.

Joe: And Vogel had a machine, I think he called it the Omega Five. I got one of his machines.

Phil: They're all CGS meters.

Joe: And they are CGS meters.. and I got a hold of your unit and I've uh.. I had a hell of a time keeping it.

Phil: CGS is a good name for it. Centimeters grams per second. You just described it you know. Real simple. It always works. About the only expensive thing in my meters is the two coils at fifty dollars a coil. They have to be wound in Germany. The Germans are the only ones that wind good coils. So I just get the coils from Germany because they have to be perfectly matched.

Joe: Jordaine Boyce was doing the same thing with the iron that you were doing over a hundred years ago. But, he was measuring it with a wheatstone bridge. And he was trying to get the efficiency between the two.

Phil: Yeah, that's right. That's all a CGS meter is a primitive CGS meter.

Joe: That's all it is. It's a primitive CGS meter.

Phil: It's a CGS with a wheatstone bridge.. I'm not lying when I say there's a little bit of difference, but not much.

Joe picks up a photograph of a B-24 and brings it in view for the video camera

Phil: (**smiling**) That's my aircraft. I'm real proud of that. The B-24. I parachuted out that thing. I wouldn't parachute out a B-17.. the bomb bay wasn't big enough. You could almost hit your head on the side of the thing when you went out. I jumped behind German lines two times I think. I got out of it every time and they couldn't figure it. (**chuckles**) I'm still cheatn' death.

Joe: See I don't think I could get out of a B-24.. the fellow, the equipment man, Tournegit had ah...no, it's a B-25..

Phil: Torunegit I think his name was. It was a B-24

Joe: No, it's a B-25.

Phil: A B-25 is a little bitty plane.

Joe: A B-25 is so oily and noisy.. it's scary.

Phil: It's a monster. A B-25 is twice as noisy as that big ol' thing. That big ol' thing is quiet.

Joe: A B-25.. I flew one from Tucson to Phoenix.. and I was a Christian by the time I got to Phoenix.

Phil: What you want to do is sit in the radio compartment. You gotta crawl through the tunnel. Yeah, I was back in the radio compartment a lot of the time when I flew in those things. There was no way out of it. Everybody would parachute outta there but the radio man. He was just stuck there. So, that's where I hid.

Joe: Took you to the top.

Phil: Every time I got stuck in a B-25 I'd say the Rosary.

Joe: Makes a Christian outta you.

Phil: Yeah, made a Christian out of me, you're dead by then. I hated that thing. (**points to the picture**) That was the B-24.

Joe: They called that the "Liberator".

Phil: The Liberator is a B-24, yeah. The B-24 Liberator...

Joe: ..and the two tails.

Phil: Best plane ever made. That thing.. if you lose three engines you could still land it. You can land that thing with one engine. It had four engines on 'em.. you could land with one engine.

Joe: It had a glide path.

Phil: Yeah, (**stretches his arm straight out to demonstrate**) It had a twelve degree glide path so it could settle down. Twelve degree angle was real easy. You know, you could cut the power off.. I cut it off a couple times, but never landed it with the power off. I almost had to land it like that.. powerless, it wasn't in too great a shape.

Joe: Halstead was really worried about the terrorists affecting our water and food.

Phil: Yeah, that figures.

Joe: And the food's coming in from Mexico and other places and they got the DDT's it that we were supplying to them down there.

Phil: In Mexico, they threw DDT around like it's nothing and they still do.

Joe: And, he was worried about what was happening to the future generations of people.. our kids and our kid's kids.

Phil: It wreaks havoc on our reproductive systems.. in Mexico that's for sure. Paramagnetism fixes the reproductive system of insects and it'll sure do it on people too if you give it a chance. Otherwise, the DDT eventually causes sterilization.

Joe: Mrs. Carson wrote the book "A Silent Spring". Rachel Carson.

Phil: Silent Spring, yeah.

Joe: I think the thing that really caught the people was the fact about what it was doing to birds.

Phil: Really important, yeah, that did it. Everybody loves birds. That did it. But birds...

Joe: ..the way birds go is about the way civilization is going to go too. I believe that if the.. if when we were talking about the canaries in the mines.. there's a possibility that birds can tell you what to eat and what water to drink..

Phil: .. Sure, sure.

Joe: ..and the air that we're breathing

Phil: When I go out in the woods, I don't.. I don't usually take much with me. I just watch what the birds eat and I just eat the same thing. You can get it anywhere, grass seeds.. I'm real big on grass seed. You just shake the seed off and throw it into a tin cup, build a fire, and make a mush out of it. I lived for weeks and weeks in Germany taking no food at all. I just lived on grass seed.

Joe: Sounds a little like Yule Gibbons doesn't it...

Phil: Yeah, (**chuckles**)

Joe: But anyway, you went on your expeditions and had practically nothing with you. You just took a tiny little survival packet. Why don't you describe your survival packet?

Phil: Yeah, yeah.. I had that little knap sack.. I still got it somewhere. It's that little blue nap sack.. it weighed about.. I never carried more than twenty pounds in it. All I had in it was a down jacket so I wouldn't freeze to death. And a trowel, a garden trowel for diggin' up insects, grubs. That's really all I carried in it was a tin cup and a down jacket and a garden trowel, probably weighed four or five pounds.

Joe: You never took any defense weapons? You never take a knife?

Phil: No. I had a pocket knife for whittl'n and mostly I'd use it to whittle sticks. If I wanted to roast something, I'd whittle a stick out and put a point on it. Oh, I still got my pocket knife somewhere.

Joe: I'd seen a Swiss knife on top of the..

Phil stands up and finds the knife on the top shelf of a book case not more than three feet away. As he describes the knife, he opens out each part of the knife. The camera zooms with a close shot of books on the middle shelves. Books titles that can be seen indicate birds, parrots, birds of prey, and flacons.

Phil: I still got it. It's got everything you need on it. It's got a blade. It's got a cork screw in case you got a bottle of champagne. It's got a phillips screw driver. Everything's got phillips heads on it. It's got a regular screw driver. It's got a can opener. It's a Swiss army knife.. that's it. That's all you need is a Swiss army knife and a tin cup. (**he folds the last part of the knife in**)

Joe: They won't even let you get on an airplane with that anymore.

Phil: No.. no.. what I do is.. I usually put it into my little.. I got a little sack I usually carry.

He places his hand over to the right side of his hip where it would go, then he stands up again to show where he places the knife

Phil: I put it in there and they just throw it in the luggage compartment. It goes through that machine and when they say there's a knife, I say it's going in the luggage compartment.. it's no problem. They just throw it in the luggage compartment and give it back to me when I leave. There's no problem with the airlines. They're reasonable. I never have any trouble with them. I don't care it's in the luggage compartment.. they never lost anything of mine.

Joe: You ever been in a place you didn't think you wouldn't get out? You ever been really close to God?

Phil: Yeah, yeah. Three times I bailed out over Germany occupied France. I thought I wouldn't get out, but I did. Usually I'd steal a jeep. I'd bail out and do what I had to do. And mostly collect data and send it back to headquarters. Then I'd just steal a jeep. The biggest ride I've had was from Munich to Marleena and back to my radio station from Marleena. It was 652 miles. I figured I.. one time I went from Marleena the other way. I went from Marleena to Balleek which was three miles. From Balleek I went to Bellfast. From Bellfast I went to Larean which is off the coast of Ireland where I cross over the wall around to Scotland which is a strand that rises over the port of Scotland. From there I went to Manchester, England then south to Bilburg. And then from their I'd cross the English Channel from Bilburg to Catileigh.

Joe: You were in hostile country there in England. I mean there were the Irish, the English, the Scots and everybody that was fightn'..

Phil: Yeah, well I was on the border there.. that was IRA. They hated my guts. The IRA there was about.. well, every teenager born to the IRA was dangerous, but they wouldn't tell you because that was a big deal. But fifteen or twenty of them were and they were fanatics.. they tried to kill me.. two or three times.

Joe: Your job there was to maintain contact with the pilots using radio beams in order to guide them back safely.

Phil: It was a 100 thousand watt radio station sitting up on the E mount. The transmitters were as big as that wall there (**Points behind Joe**). They were huge and they had coils in them like that (**forms a circle almost the size of a hula hoop with both his long arms**). Very dangerous.

Joe: You were all there by yourself.. no help.

Phil: No help at all.

Joe: It would ice up.. you had to knock all that ice off.

Phil: When you were a radio commando, you'd train as a radio commando.. that's your job. If anybody tried to knock it off you'd have to kill 'em. You'd keep going and kill anyone that tries to knock it off the air.

Joe: The German's tried to triangulate you and tried to find you all the time.

Phil: Oh yeah, they tried it.. they'd try to find me. I outwitted the Germans. I outwitted Germans and the IRA. They tried to find the station all the time. I had a parrot that would start saying "how you doing" as soon as anyone got close. And when the parrot would start saying "how you doing" I'd just go out in the woods. I had my forty five. Took it in my bag here (**points to his hip**). I never used it. The Germans would come by and look at it [the radio station] they wouldn't even know what it was they were so stupid. The Nazis would come look at it and never blew it up.. they didn't know what it was. They thought it was a broadcast station for the news. They thought we were puttin' out news for Good Morning America or something (**chuckles**).

Joe: I don't know if I understand you or not, but the Germans would send out two beams and when the German planes would fly they'd find those beams and could zero in where they crossed and that's where they dropped their bombs.

Phil: (**points his two index fingers outward and crosses one over the other**) So what I did was send out another beam so that it crossed over the country side in cow pastures where they dropped all their bombs. They never hit London. They never dropped a single bomb on London.

Joe: And all of it was secret. You'd never tell anyone about what you were doing because..

Phil: As soon as I get the Medal of Honor we'd probably find out that the British were gonna give me a Victorian Cross and the Jewish people were gonna give me a medal for shooting if I ever get a document out of them or so. I drove six-hundred and fifty-two miles from Marleena to Germany and crashed through the gates of Dactou Germany. I remember I did it and came back all through enemy territory.

Joe: (**chuckles**) Well things got boring and you come back and "marry your girl" as the English put it.. or your misogynist used to say.. Anyway, you put it off for a couple years and you roamed around the world.. she waited for you.

Phil: Yeah, yeah, walked around the world.. thirty three thousand miles. I figured it out.. it was thirty three thousand miles I walked. This fellow here was with me. This Jewish fellah..

(gets up and pulls a picture from behind Joe. Joe holds the photograph in view of the video camera)

..Colonel Blesney and I.. of course he couldn't go through the middle east. He was Jewish, so they wouldn't give him a visa, and so I crossed the middle east myself, but I met him back in London. He's my closest friend.. he and I hiked around the world together except the middle east. I was by myself there. I walked with Ken Silver and Irwin Pless all over Europe. I met Ken at the railroad station in London and Irwin in Japan. He was a radio navigation systems expert in Japan. We were both radio navigators and built the systems for Collins Electronics in Iowa.

Joe: Well, you went just to observe. To see what you wanted to see.. to see how people lived.

Phil: I learned more from the Arabs and the Bedouins than anybody. The Bedouins lived in the desert on nothin'. That's where I learned most about the desert.

Joe: Don't you remember what Green said?

Marilyn: He said his grandfather was a Bedouin. He said he'd love you and his grandfather to get together. He figured you two would get along fine even if you couldn't understand each other. He said you reminded him of his grandfather.

Phil: You go into a Bedouin camp and eat yourself to death (chuckles). You know they give you the goat's eye. I never liked that too much.. the eye didn't taste all that good. They'd kill a goat.. the eye was a delicacy. More than once I had to kind of hide it (**shows how he would get rid of it behind his back**).

Joe: (laughs) Hide it behind your back!

Phil: (**Chuckles**) But that's what they always gave when they welcomed guests.

Joe: They get by with very little water. They didn't have much sanitation yet they're pretty healthy people.

Phil: They know about paramagnetism. They do the same thing I did.. put some paramegnetic rock in a canteen and it wouldn't evaporate anymore. They used paramagnetic rocks to keep the water from evaporating.

Joe: The Romans took magnetite, Fe_3O_4, and put it inside their troughs that they were delivering their water with.

Phil: Sure, no evaporation. They put it in the bottom of the troughs. They knew that from watching streams, they could see that not much water would evaporate from streams. They found when the rocks were out of the irrigation ditches the water would evaporate. So, they'd put rocks into the bottom of the irrigation ditches.. it would stop the water from evaporating.

Joe: Very few people picked up on what you were doing on paramegnetic attraction to water. And, yet, the deserts could benefit from that more than anybody else.

Phil: Well that's the beauty of how God takes care of things. I won't even talk about stuff like when they give me a Medal of Honor. They won't make a paramagnetic speech. Then it'd get all over the world and then everybody'd believe it. No problem (smiles). See, they don't experiment.. if I go to the Warren experiment station and give a lecture, they'd believe it, but when it gets in a book they don't believe it.

Joe: How could they not believe it when you look at Tucson and how desert it is. It's got twelve inches of water a year. Look over here.. you got twelve inches of water and look, everything is green.

Phil: It's green as can be. Tucson doesn't absorb paramagnetics. Around here there's no desert. It's green forest with small trees. (**points out the window**) Those trees are only about thirty feet high most of them. They grow out but don't grow up. They grow outward.

Joe: In Mexico, let's say, Guaymas.. Guaymas has the same rain and the same temperature as Hawaii. But Hawaii's got all this green and everything else.

Phil: It's all magnetic. Hawaii is a paramagnetic volcanic island.

Joe: It's paramagnetic volcanic ash.

Phil: All you gotta do.. it's common sense to take a look at Hawaii and say it's volcanic. Then you go get the rocks and see what's in it. I invented the word paramagnetism because it's a weak magnetic field. Para means weak.

Joe: Paramagnetics is a balance. It's not about the north pole or the south pole.. it's about the balance of life.

Phil: It's the balance of Ying and Yang as the Chinese used to call it.. called it biomagnetism or paramagnetism. Ying and Yang, up and down, to the Chinese Yang is female magnetism and Ying is the male.

Joe: It's so confusing. To the English.. everything they write about.. the north pole is the south pole and the south pole is the north pole and if you try to read universal stuff you can get mixed up pretty easy.

Miniature ceramic representation of Biddy Early's house

Phil: Our terminology got all mixed up and it drives people crazy, so they just give up on it. Cause if you read one book, it's got the English terminology, and the other one has the American, and yet another one has the French so you kinda of give up on it. (**Phil turns towards Joe and points to miniature hand sized houses made of kiln fired clay**) Those little houses.. one of them is paramagnetic and that one is Biddy Early's house. Biddy

Early was one of the greatest healers that ever lived.. there's no question about that. It survived many years preserved like that and a couple generations later they came along and just tore it down. But, she was probably the greatest healer that ever lived. She had a blue bottle and put rocks in it. Of course the sun would hit the bottle and the blue light would energize the rock. Then she'd give that to people and it would heal them. So that's how I figured out she was healing people. If you go to Ireland, everybody'll tell you who Biddy Early is. They'd say, "Oh, she's a healer". She learned it all from sitting at the face of a rock and she knew it was magical. She'd take a little piece of paramagnetic rock and put it in the bottle. When she died, she threw the blue bottle in the middle of a lake. It sunk in the mud, but I spent a week down there looking for that bottle. I never found it.. it's down there in the sand no doubt.

Joe: The blue bottle would be more likely cobalt, wouldn't it?

Phil: Cobalt is what it was. It was a cobalt bottle.

Joe: So, that goes back to Tesla's testing using cobalt coatings on aluminum.. Ying and Yang.

Phil: The ancient people put cobalt in the blue bottles because they knew it would make the water healthy. So all the blue bottles were made with cobalt. Still are.

Joe: Goes clear back to the eye of Alexander doesn't it.

Phil: Yeah. I got a blue bottle around here somewhere.

Joe: It's up on top (**Joe points the video camera to the top of the book shelf. It is a square shaped cobalt blue bottle**) the eye of Alexander was cobalt. After that, the Egyptians worshiped blue.

Phil: Blue was the sacred color for the Egyptians and Mesopotamians in general.

Joe: The royalty too.

Phil: The royalty and everybody. All that stuff was in the ancient religion. That picture up there.. I bought it.. it was by a famous Japanese artist. I found it for sale for about a hundred bucks at some store and somebody told me it was worth thirty or forty thousand dollars. Japan's most famous woodcut artist.. and the only way I knew it was real was because I read in some ancient literature that the women used to get those for gift cards on their birthday. You'd get those on your birthday.. they'd fold it into four and put it in their pocket. That's why there four creases on that.

Joe: That's how you can tell it's real.

Phil: Yeah, that's how you can tell. I bought that for a couple hundred dollars and took it into the museum in Tokyo and they said, "oh, it's probably worth fifteen or twenty thousand."

Joe: Now, paramagnetic stone that's fed to gardens.. plants can take the life energy from that while it travels within the innards.

Phil: It goes right up the flow up the cortex and the outer layers of the plant. Most of it is in the outer layer. The outer layer is the bark and the inner layer is the cortex.

Joe: Dr. Rickets took your paramagnetics and lignites and mixed it together to grew carrots and radishes. He would get eight and nine hundred percent more vitamins and minerals. And the iron oxide..

Phil: ..It takes your vitamins and makes them ten times better.

Joe: So, most of the food we're getting now has one tenth the vitamins and minerals.

Phil: That's why you're better off eating green vegetables. Vegetables used to have vitamins, but now only your organics have them. Most of the vegetables grown are organic green vegetables, so most of it is safe. This country has gone organic.

Joe: When iron oxide gets into these plants it becomes collective of solar energy. It becomes hot. Paramagnetic iron oxide gets ten times hotter than any other dirt or soil around it. So, that energy is transferred.

Phil: That's why if you take one of these little balls and roll it around in your hands it gets hot. It's not your hand warming the ball.. it's the ball warming your hand. It takes energy right out of the atmosphere.

Joe: We were talking about this lady that was taking paramagnetic rocks and putting it in a blue bottle. It would then structure the water.

Phil: Yeah, the sunlight enters the bottle passing through the cobalt blue glass and energizes the water that surrounds the paramagnetic rock. The sunlight in the room.. it doesn't matter if it's inside or out, enters the bottle and stores energy in the paramagnetic water. It's like a radio system.. it stores it. The radio has stored energy. It puts a signal up to the transmission station, stores it, then puts it right back down. All electronics have stored energy.

Joe: Energy, we're not really measuring it at all. There's probably more energies than we realize out there. There's fifth energies and sixth energies.

Phil: I discovered another one.. it's called paramagnetics. They didn't even know much about that.. they didn't know it existed. It's a weak electromagnetic energy that nobody considers. I named it paramagnetics because it's like a parachute. It's a weak thing.. parachutes don't weigh much, but it'll keep you from getting killed when you jump out of an airplane. It's a weak energy.

Joe: Now, when you heat paramagnetic energy at high temperatures, it changes. It doesn't have the magnetic attraction, but there's still another energy there. What's that one?

Phil: It's infra red. No question about that. When you heat it up you generate infra red. You got paramagnetism that is a transmitter and infra red is the signal that's going out. Paramagnetism is an object itself. What it does is takes the infra red energy that comes out in the infra red spectrum.. so you got sixty two angstroms, eighty two angstroms, ninety nine point six, sixty two point eight angstroms. You get them all lined up and you'll find out that those are the ones that are all healthy. You get the wrong ones and you find they're poisons. (**Phil raises his hands and brings them together aligning his fingers from his left to the right. He's demonstrating an alignment when he shifts the fingers of both hands slightly spun off center to show a misalignment**)... these are the angstroms that are tuned and these are the ones out of mesh.

Joe: That's what Halstead was worried about.. that these terrorists got the tunement and could actually take a frequency and put a plate underneath an aspirin bottle then tell you what aspirin was in the bottle. But they could also tune it to a bad frequency making it poisonous.

Phil: Yeah, you can take any medicine and put into a blue bottle and place it in the sun. If you sit by it, it'll cure you just as fast as taking it.

Marilyn: You said cure you, not kill you...

Phil: Cure you, well if it's a good energy, like perfume, it'll cure you, but if it's a toxic frequency, it'll injure you.

Joe: Now, so this is going to Pasteur's work.

Phil: He didn't know the physics of it, but he knew what he was doing.

Joe: He called it memory.

Phil: Everything has memory. That plate on the wall there has memory.

Joe: If you're cleaning water.. dirty water won't pick up memory.. it has to be clean water, but if it's paramagnetic clean water that's run over iron crystals, then it'll capture an image just like audio and visual tapes.

Phil: You can take a laser and focus it on the image of the falcon on the plate there (**Phil points to a decorative plate across the room**) and the image will float right out here in the room. Yeah, you can take a laser which is coherent energy which means the waves are going out together instead of separately. You can point that at any picture and that energy.. that picture will float out here in the room.

Joe: That's why you point a laser at the moon you want concentrated in a straight line.

Phil: When a laser leaves the Earth it's about a millimeter across, but when it gets to the moon it's about an inch across. It doesn't expand any.. it doesn't spread much. Atmosphere scatters the photons which is why it spreads a little.

Joe: So when Dr. Benson was working on.. he had to use quartz lenses or lights or tubes, he put the magnets on the back side and then put the magnetite iron on to the side and then shot the laser through the quartz.. he couldn't do it through glass.. he had to use quartz.

Phil: Had to do it through quartz because glass won't work. Glass is a mixture of everything and quartz is pure is a pure crystal.

Joe: So he's got the frequencies going right through the end of the iron and when the water flowed over the iron it would clean it. Now he told me one thing. He said, "Joe go drill a hole in the top of a pipe on the road somewhere close to this and put a piece of Gore-Tex [polytetrafluoro-ethylene, or PTFE]. He said Gore-Tex will let the gas go, but it won't let the water go through.

Phil: That all came from me. I used to fill polyethylene tubes with it and drive it in the ground to grow big trees and plants. You can drive the tubes into kiln fired pots or in the ground to grow your your plants that way. I had a garden like that one time.

Joe: I can't remember the fellows name, but he had a place called Union Gardens he called it.

Phil: Hugh Lowell is his name.

Joe: Yeah, Lowell had some of the most beautiful stuff I'd seen in my life. What he was doing was taking rusty pipes, closing the bottom end and filling it half way with magnetite with a crystal in the middle, and filling the rest to the top. And at the top he had a screw and would turn that down putting pressure on it. He had some of the most beautiful plants I'd ever seen in my life.

Phil: I did talks on that.

Joe: I know you know the man. He's from Brightonsville, Georgia, and he's got Union Gardens.

Phil: What's his name.. I can't think of his name.

Joe: I'm trying to think of his name too.

Phil: Connors or something..

Joe: Connors was that woman.. no, that was right next door, Connors is that woman who had those visions.

Phil: Yeah, but her name.. Nancy Fowler was her name.

Joe: Nancy Fowler. I went over and visited two or three days with her, and they had a migration come over there of Catholics from all over the world. They had so many people that they didn't have any place for them to go to the bathroom. So, they brought in close to fifty toilets.. port-a-potties, and there were people arriving in Greyhound buses from thousands of miles around. She was a very simple woman.. very nice.

Phil: She was a close friend of mine. I'll bet they tried to shut her down. When I went up there, he changed his mind in a hurry and started preaching about her.

Joe: I was impressed by her.

Phil: Oh, she's for real.

Joe: Christopher Bird lived just a little ways from there. Remember when I brought those papers from there?

Marilyn: And her message was very simple too.

Winnie: Very very simple.

Joe: I really.. I was so impressed with her. And there were all these people coming in on busses.. it must have made her mad.. there must've been a couple hundred buses.

Winnie: And they all wanted to see her.

Joe: They all wanted to see her.

Phil: And all you had to do was be yourself and quit being uptight.. just by playful like it's a big game.

Joe: Now, she didn't have any special education.. it's as if she was tuning in..

Winnie: She was tuning into God.

Marilyn: She is a nurse.

Phil: She was a nurse.

Joe: I told you I had these pads that I made with paramagnetics and I took them to the hospice where people were dying. I took hundreds of them to these people. They liked them.. particularly if I put 'em in the freezer to get 'em cold. I'd seal them because if I didn't, they'd stink. The doctors would come along and throw them away.

Phil: The chemical doctors.

Joe: And the nurses too.. nobody would ever believe that there's something about these energies. Particularly if you take and set it in the sun.. and one thing about them that you told me is, you wash them in sea water. Now I'm not talking processed salt.. sea salt.

Phil: Sea salt. Health food store has sea salt.

Joe: And something I found out when you put seaweed with it.. you take and pulverize the seaweed.. there's something about the kelp with the iodine and a couple other things with it.

Phil: Seaweed is the best, and of course the Irish farmers would get it from the coast where it was, break it up and dry it out, then spread it out on their fields.

Joe: Seaweed mixes great when you sonically grind it and mix it with iron oxide and lignites… you can't believe the way it grows.

Phil: It's all common sense. The ancient people knew all this.

Joe: Seaweed works best without being washed. Don't ever wash the salt off it. Leave the salt right on it.

Phil: You leave the seaweed alone. It's common sense is all it is.

Joe: Explain the sonic grounding I'm doing it with.

Phil: Well, you're not actually touching it with something like a hammer you're getting more pure iron than you need. When the iron comes off the hammer or whatever is used to pulverize the iron oxide, molecules come off the metal head and contaminate the magnetite making it too strong. When you use ultra sonics you're not touching or upsetting anything. The material stays more natural. Stick with nature.

Joe: You're staying with nature.. staying with balance.

Phil: That bird you hear chirping is not the chirping. It's the ultrasonics it's putting out to me. But I don't talk in ultrasonics so the bird's wondering why I don't talk back. When I go in there and run the water from the faucet, the water passing over the iron from within the pipe puts out ultrasonics and the bird will start talking like mad.

Joe: Now if you took a crystal, like a bowl with crystals there and put water over it, it would intensify the sound.

Phil: It would intensify the ultrasonics and that bird will start talking to you. It's not the sonics a bird pays attention to, it's the ultrasonics.

Joe: When you take these iron oxides, the Fe_3O_4 particularly, the high gauss CGS of nineteen thousands.. sprinkle a little around where people have sprayed for insects.. what's happening?

Phil: Well what happens is the good stuff happens. In other words, God has created the earth so there's good and the bad. The bad is the insects that don't belong there and the good are the parasites and predators that eat off the insects which destroy your crop. So actually, you want them because they're the good insects. When you put down paramagnetism, you'll attract the good insects and repel the bad ones. That's the way God designed it. I don't know why, it just seems that's the way God designed it that way. The bad insects just disappear. If you take what like I got near my window sill... (**Phil gets up from his chair and moves towards his window**)

Joe: What are you looking for?

Phil: I had one there. This little rock. I just put an antenna on it.

Joe: Oh, look at that Marilyn. I pick these up every time I go to the store because I put paramagnetic soil on them, but I didn't put an antenna on it. See, I learn something every time I come.

Phil: (**Phil takes the plastic cap off of a 3 inch long white prescription like container**) This is paramagnetic rock with a nail in it.

Joe: See Marilyn, the nail or the screw goes right down through it and it's got an antenna on top.

Phil: The antenna makes it about ten times stronger.

Joe: Now, the guy would take this and fill it with iron oxide, the Fe_3O_4 and put it around anywhere you need to diffuse weak field magnetics...

Phil: You can put this in your room and you'll never get sick.

Joe: You put that by a TV or anywhere you have radiation.

Phil: You put that by the TV and that's the end of the bad radiation.

Winnie: But it also keeps the ants out.

Joe: would it be better with copper or just regular steel?

Phil: Copper or anything. It doesn't matter.

Marilyn: It also keeps the ants out you said too?

Phil: I've never seen an ant.

Winnie: Ants don't come in anymore even at the door.

Joe: Marilyn's got them all over the house. I can see that now!

Phil: All you gotta do is go out and get pieces of paramagnetic rock or granite or basalt, whatever, and put a nail with it. You don't even need the antenna on it.. I just put it there to pick up the container.

Joe: Now, I put crystals in with the iron oxide.. and I put those together..

Phil: That'd make it even better..

Joe: And what about when you squeeze it.. put a little pressure on it?

Phil: When you put pressure on it, it's called the piezoelectric effect and it gets stronger. piezoelectric effect generates electricity so you're putting energy into it. It's like an electric generator, like a motor. It even drives insects away from ten yards off.

Joe: Those little balls I made over there.. I could actually put a pin in them or do anything else to make an antenna on them.

Phil: Yeah, an ordinary straight pin.

Joe: In the hyperbaric chamber with sodium silicate.. that's quartz crystals isn't it?

Phil: You just drive a stainless steel pin in it and it becomes ten times stronger. We don't get those sugar ants anymore because it's too strong. They don't like to go where there's high paramagnetism and keep away from it. But, if you go out to a harvester ant hill, they cut the leaves so they can get them down and the leaves slowly ferment of which they feed from. If you go to the harvester ant hill, you'll notice the mound is white and pink. The ants bring quartz and pink granite pebbles ant by ant and cover the whole ant hill with the stones. So, you've got a paramagnetic and diamagnetic hood over the cone of the mound. It's a paramagnetic layer that covers the ant hill. If you go out here about a half a mile, there's a harvester ant hill and if you look at it, it's white and pink. It's just common sense.. ask yourself, "what does the ant do?"

Joe: You just had a good thing there.. a blue bottle with a couple energy balls.. put it in the sun..

Phil: ..in the sun..

Joe: ..and drink the water.

Phil: ..and drink the water and you'll never get sick. You put these around the house and never get a cold.. whatever you call a cold (laughs).

Joe: Now, what if you took one of those metallic möbius' that Tesla was talking about, for instance, that was made out of audio video tape. You put a möbius inside that and tap it with a nail. Is that what you're talking about?

Phil: If you make it counterclockwise it'll be good, but if it's clockwise it'll probably ruin you.

Joe: Counterclockwise..

Phil: ..counterclockwise, yes.

Joe: That's exactly what Tesla said. "To the left... always to the left."

Phil: The Irish people for centuries.. they don't do it anymore.. I don't know why, but if you took a church, like the one at Nock where that statue is from which is a paramagnetic limestone church, they would warn you to never walk around it clockwise. They walked around it counter-clockwise. Never walk clockwise because it would make you feel sick. Still does.. if you walk around that church clockwise.. I did it one time to see and ended up sick to my stomach. I was throwing up all night long.

Joe: The Indians have these medicine wheels and they always go to the left. Nobody's ever understood this.. if you take a möbius and turn it upside down it should be opposite, but it isn't.

Phil: No, because it's got a hundred and eighty degree twist in it. It's got no one side to it because it's an infinite loop.

Joe: There's no up or down on it. When you drill a hole in a möbius, where does the energy go from?

Phil: The energy probably separates and goes around the hole. Some of it might fall in the hole, like a hole in a water pipe, not much though because the energy's too fast just like water goes around a hole in a fast stream, it doesn't go down except for some.

Joe: If you were to wrap one of these as a capacitor with the gold foil, would that intensify it?

Phil: Yeah, if you wrapped it to the left. If you wrapped it to the right it'll probably make you sick. If it's counterclockwise it'd probably cancel the effect of being sick from one that was wrapped clockwise.

Joe: The mind.. you're doing this with your mind and the fact that your mind is doing it to the left. Do you think the human mind has something to do with the energizing aspect?

Phil: Doctors know that.. that your left mind is your thinking side. Your left side of the brain is the side that reasons. The right side is the one for language. Your right side memorizes like for language and your left side reasons. They've known that for a hundred years. Tesla said that. He realized he was thinking with the left side of his brain.

Joe: I gave you one piece of paper there. I saw Syd's paper on that and he quoted me on it. Tesla said that the only way we could protect ourselves from detrimental magnetic fields was to use a metallic möbius wound to the left.

Phil: Everything in nature that works is designed counterclockwise. Once you go against the energy of the sun it becomes excess energy. You can't handle it so you make sure it goes on the left side of the brain there.

Joe: These little things can be tested so easily... using birds for example..

Phil: The reason why people are so sensitive is because they have an excess on the left side of the brain.

Marilyn: I have a question about direction.. is that also true south of the equator?

Phil: There's a big debate going on now and the way I... every time I fly south of the equator which isn't anymore, I don't know if the airplane was canceling it, but I didn't get any real difference, except one time I was in the jungles of the equator, I got the impression.. I didn't stay there long and I didn't have my CGS meter with me either so I couldn't make sure.. but, I got the impression if you stayed at the equator.. if you went around in clockwise circles, you'd get sick. I didn't stay there long enough, but I had the impression I didn't feel as good.

Joe: I'll have to check that one out.

Marilyn: But, if you went south of the equator..

Phil: South of the equator it's the opposite..

Marilyn: So, south of the equator you'd want to go around the church clockwise.

Phil: Clockwise, right.

Marilyn: Okay, that's what I was wondering.

Joe: On our fortieth anniversary, our kids gave us a boat and we got down to the point where the boat was using seawater to flush the toilets. I went in there to use the toilets and when I flushed, it went the wrong way. So, I spent an hour sittin' there looking at it flushing.. I got myself a bottle of booze and watched it go 'round and 'round. I thought I'd lost my marbles.

Phil: You gotta be careful because of the natives and headhunters south of the equator. I had a hard time trying to explain to them, but they wanted to do the opposite of what I was talking about. I finally got to the point. Robyn or Raymond.. I can't think of his name at the moment.. Robyn was a scientist.. Raymond was a famous shaman among the headhunters. He was a friend of mine and probably the funniest part of it was.. I had a Cessna two fifty and the pilot was a major in the Peruvian Air force. I was a copilot of course and the shaman wanted to fly. So we got him in the plane, but when it started, he was terrified. He got in the back seat and huddled there and we finally had to land him in a cow pasture. We thought he was gonna die. He was so afraid of that thing. He wanted to be in it so bad but then we had to land in a clearing and let him out (laughs). He said he'd rather walk back home. And he did (all laugh). He had about a twenty mile walk.

Joe: Burt told me one time that.. he was talking about some people.. the indians.. that there'd be Spanish boats that would come into the harbor.. the Indians would look at them but couldn't see them. They never had anything to relate to that boat so they couldn't see it. Not until they took them out on a boat littler than that and take them to the ship and after that they could see it.

Phil: That happened to me with birds. Some birds you can't relate to cause you really don't like them. Sittin' right in front of them and you can't really see them. Bird watchers sometimes tell me, "How come you always see a hawk, but you never see hawks?" Well, because subconsciously you don't like hawks because hawks kill other birds, so you don't see them. But I can see a hawk now in the corner of my eye. It can be a couple miles up in the air and I'll still see it.

Joe: I was down in Brazil one time and there was a tree sitting out on the plain and it had these beautiful leaves I've ever seen in my life. They were florescent. So I took this land rover and drove over to it and as I got near all the leaves flew away. It was a dead tree. Something shocked the hell out of them.. the leaves just blew away!

Phil: The birds were sittin' on it. They love those trees. Hawks always pick on that tree. I used to when I was younger about sixteen or seventeen.. I would hardly ever look for hawks nests.. I'd just get a little white mouse and put him in a wire cage and make a hundred loops using wire. A wild hawk would come down to get the mouse and get caught in the wire loops. I'd take the hawk and tame it. Most people never get them tamed, but I can in three days. I could tame a hawk and it would be a perfectly wild one. Sometimes you'd lose them because they get out of sight and you couldn't find them. I'd never bother with looking for the nest, I'd trap them in Ireland and just train 'em. I'd trap kestrels, but I didn't want to hunt birds anyway. I'd trap rats and mice instead. Kestrels hunt rats and mice. There's a book around here an English friend of mine wrote. I was just reading it this morning. It's somewhere here near the couch. There it is.. "Lure of the Falcon".

Joe: I read your books. I think I know everything I know about your books, but I read them over and over and there's always something that I miss.. that I always pass by. I'll pick up something after the tenth or twelfth time or whatever. There's something there that wasn't there before.

Phil: That's why I write 'em. A lot of people interested in nature.. they love my books. They buy 'em. Acres can't quit printing them.

Joe: I wish the old man's eyes would get a little bit better.

Phil: Yeah, that's a shame. Chuck Walters is a genius in agriculture.. an agricultural genius if there ever was one.

Joe: I hadn't seen him in a little bit and I was up there.. I can't.. it's just hard to believe he's going blind.

Phil: I tried to tell him to use a little paramagnetic rock in his orange juice. I don't know why people don't listen. I told him, "if you put a little ground up paramagnetic rock in your orange juice it'll probably cure you." He never did.

Joe: Oh, what if I took a quartz tube, like a test tube, with paramagnetic nineteen thousand CGS, and even seal it at the top and put that in there.. would the vibrational frequencies go through quartz.

Phil: I usually put it in plastic tubes, but quartz would be a lot better. Plastic is diamagnetic and quartz would be stronger and you wouldn't need a nail any more. It would be just too strong and you wouldn't need a nail.. it'd be so powerful it would cure anything.

Joe: If you took a copper coil in there and coiled it to the left and put it up like an antenna.

Phil: It would make it a little better.. probably make it an eighth or a quarter better.

Joe: Silver or gold?

Phil: Silver or gold would make it a little better.. by a quarter or stronger.

Joe: If you put a little pressure on the crystals...

Phil: It would make it better. Clamp it using a little pressure, not a lot. You'd have a powerful healing device.

Joe: We're talking about several different energies aren't we.

Phil: That's piezoelectric energy there. You can imagine piezoelectric energy to infra red energy.. all transistors work that way.. transistors are piezoelectric.. So, that's the transmitter, and what comes out is electrical energy as a radio wave. That's what works in an airplane you talk about a vacuum.. if you stop to think mathematically using a little integrated calculus, the vacuum the plane couldn't possibly get off the ground. The plane is so heavy and the vacuum is so weak it wouldn't work. That's what's in all the books. The electrical and aeronautical engineers say it can't work because there's not enough energy and I'd say, "well, look at this.." and I plugged in some calculus formulas on the board to show how it worked. The airplane is made out of aluminum and the skin of the plane is cloth.. that's diamagnetic, and oxygen is paramagnetic, then the whole thing lift.

Joe: What if you put little scales like on fish?

Phil: That's why the fish can move upstream. They use paramagnetic and diamagnetic energies.

Joe: What if you put some on a model airplane?

Phil: Well, they'd probably levitate in the air.. the fish would float above the tank and they wouldn't stay in the water (**Joe and Phil laugh as Phil demonstrates with his hands what it would look like**). I did that once, not with fish, but I did that with a bug once. I took a needle and generated a paramagnetic force on the bottom and a diamagnetic force above it and it floated in the air. An entomologist came along and said, "Well, it's flying". Well, beetles are heavy because they have the heavy wing covers, elytra. Well, it can't be flying they say "it's too heavy.. it can't be floatin' in the air like that."

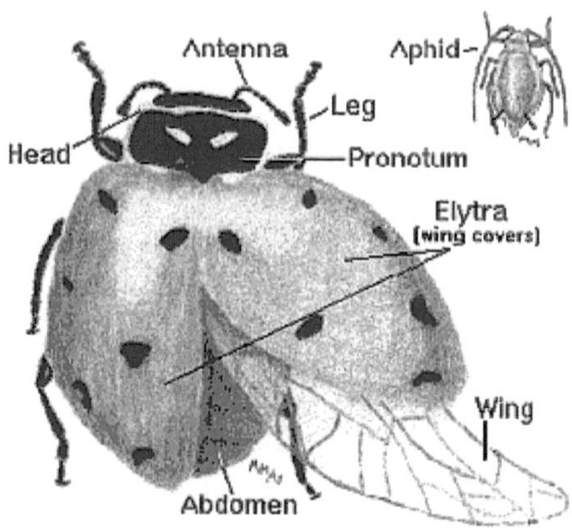

Joe: Well, they said that a june bug or a bumble bee can't fly.. aeronautically it's impossible.

Phil: They don't know about paramagnetism and diamagnetism.

Joe: You think that's why the june bug and bumble bee can fly.

Phil: The oxygen is paramagnetic and the june bug and all insects are mostly water just like people. You're mostly diamagnetic because of the water. I couldn't even measure the paramagnetism in your body because you're mostly water and that's diamagnetic. I could measure the diamagnetism real easy, but it's hard to measure the paramagnetics because there's so little of it.. you're about ninety-eight percent water, so there's just a trace of paramagnetism in your body.

Joe: What energy are these dowsers tapping into. Is it paramagnetics?

Phil: Yeah, it's paramagnetics. They take a quartz crystal on a string and can tell because your body oscillates back and forth from diamagnetism to paramagnetism. It just goes around in circles.

Joe: Now, Walter Gurniak.. you met him from Cornell.. he died this last year. He told me that if you take a cotton cloth or silk string and cover it with bee's wax..

Phil: Sure.. the cotton string is paramagnetic and the bee's wax is the magic substance. Bee's wax oscillates from paramagnetic to diamagnetic states. So, pretty soon it starts to twirl around in circles.

Joe: It's a hermaphrodite, so it goes both ways.

Phil: It goes both ways.. so is your body, it oscillates back and forth. One second it's diamagnetic and the next its paramagnetic.

Joe: That's life. Life in balance

Phil: If your body goes totally diamagnetic you're dead.

Joe: You knew Coates Perth and the psychic, Thelma Moss, who did that work for "Psychic Discoveries behind the Iron Curtain." Well, Coates has come out with a new film in the theater.. let's see if I can get you a copy of it and mail it to you.. what the hell was the name? What do we know.. what the hell do we know..?

Marilyn: What the bleep do we know.

Joe: What the bleep do we know. And in it there is a lot of people.. it's very good.. and they're talking about things we're talking about.

Winnie: Oh, that sounds interesting.

Joe: You knew Coates up at the UCLA.. I remember her in the lab, she carried her baby around with her on her back like a papoose. She's a brilliant lady.. I loved her, but I looked at her in this movie and she's old.. I haven't looked in the mirror myself.

Marilyn: There's a little story built into this movie. She did a lot of interviews with these people all through the movie.

Joe: I saw this movie and really enjoyed it. It's just that I knew a lot of people who were in it. Just thought I'd mention it because it really makes you stop and think. We really don't know much.

Phil: I knew Edgar Casey real well. He was the happiest man in the world because everybody would bad mouth him and everything else until I came along and explained it all to him. Then they stopped bad mouthing him. He used all this stuff, but didn't know how it worked until I explained it.

Joe: He got that from dreams. I never met him but I met his son. He's got a clinic in Arizona on Fortieth and Indian School and they treat people for cancer and all this other stuff. He's got a couple of medical doctors.. Mr. and Mrs. Grady. I took my mother up there before she died.

Phil: He wanted to save the Black Forest. The Black Forest, because it was non-linear, well, it wasn't a mixture of bushes and trees and plants, therefore, it got sicker and sicker. I was talking to Casey one time and he mentioned it to me. He asked about it and all I said was what I noticed about streams. Streams serpentine through the forests and all the fish are happy and all the bugs are happy and everybody's happy. So I suggested he make a big stream. He got tons of lumbar and made a trough. He collected snow water from the mountains somewhere north of the forest and sent it down the trough through the Black Forrest and it recuperated. They give him the credit for it for saving the forrest just by listening to me.

Joe: Now, the mineral that's in that water that's grinding on the snow is where the diamagnetics is showing up. What about the people in Tibet and all up in there that drink the glacier water?

Phil: Same thing.

Joe: You knew Betty Morales real well

Phil: I never met her, but I knew of her.

Joe: Betty went over there and brought back a couple jugs of water. I got in trouble during World War II when the Russians were there. I had them ship me water from all over.. the rivers and spas, and I found magnesium sulphate of all things, and that was one thing that helped kill pain. I played with water all my life.

Phil: Good water is built with chemicals that make it good.

Joe: Well, minerals, rather than chemicals..

Phil: Well, yeah, minerals of all kinds are not just chemicals. Good minerals are diamagnetic. A lot of diamagnetic minerals are good as well as sand which is diamagnetic.. so if you have the right kind of sand in a stream you have tremendous relaxation.

Joe: Quartz is diamagnetic and iron is paramagnetic.

Phil: Anything that's rust which is iron oxide of course is paramagnetic and water is diamagnetic. Most of the rocks in rivers and streams are a mixture of the two. The smooth pebbles in the stream are diamagnetic and the rough ones are paramagnetic. I always go to a stream and pick up a rock and if it's smooth it's diamagnetic and if it's rough it's paramagnetic.

Joe: You said something that I always wondered about. You can't magnetize a ball, but you can magnetize anything that's got points on it.

Phil: Anything that's rough, when you look at it under a microscope like those balls, there's lots of little points. It's like millions of antennas, so it's powerful.

Joe: I found they're more powerful when I mix sapphides with it when I grind them up. Now why would sapphides be more powerful?

Phil: Well, sapphire is highly diamagnetic. It's probably a CGS of minus two hundred instead of a minus seventy, so it's very diamagnetic. The stronger it is paramagnetic and diamagnetic the more powerful it is. If you use basalt, which is higher than pink granite for paramagnetism, it'd be even stronger. If you get up to fourteen thousand that's really strong. Basalt is about fourteen thousand which is really strong. Pink granite is only three or four thousand.

Joe:. I mixed pink granite with magnetite and I'm getting about nineteen thousand.

Phil: Pink granite is real good.

Joe: Tesla said about this granite bed. He said if you want to charge these purple plates you have to put them on a bed of granite. Then you have to use Tesla coils.. high electrical power and leave them there for at least twenty-four hours.

Phil: If you really want to charge something up you have to put more electricity into it, store it, and then cut it off. It charges and gets stored. You can charge this up (**Phil picks up the container with the paramagnetic rocks, nail, and antenna**) using a Racine motor for a couple days and it'll be ten times stronger.

Joe: I had taken this iron oxide and put it on a band-aid and then on a florescent tube where the power's coming in and it doubles the life of the tube.

Phil: Oh sure, it'll double the life of anything. It'll double your life. If you die at sixty you won't live to 120 if you had paramagnetics around you, but you'd probably reach ninety or older. If you put these in your pocket you'll never get sick.

Joe: Birds can actually peck out the paramagnetic out of the soil and eat them.

Phil: Yeah, birds know all about that.

Phil: Oh yeah, if you kill a chicken and open its crop, you'll find paramagnetic stones.

Joe: Is this why birds like parrots have such long life spans?

Phil: Yep.

Joe: What about turtles, is this why they have long life spans?

Phil: The water is going in through their nostrils. That's why turtles are so long lived because they live in a paramagnetic environment. Unless it's polluted and then they die. It's not uncommon for a turtle to live over a hundred years. I had a box turtle.. my mother got tired of it (**to Winnie**) didn't we let it go?

Winnie: You took it without telling her..

Phil: How 'bout that. I forgot about my mother. She fell in love with that turtle. It was a tortoise which is a land turtle. I wasn't even thinking of her. It'd probably live to about a hundred and fifty years old. It's probably still out there in Gainesville.

Winnie: No, we took it on the road with us.

Phil: Oh yeah, it's in a marsh somewhere in Texas. There's a lake somewhere..

Winnie: We didn't tell her we were doing it. She forgot about it.

Phil: I hoped she forgot about it.

Joe: I heard a joke one time about a fellow who sent his mother a parrot. He come home and says, "where's the parrot?" The mother says, "why?" He says, "Well, that parrot was a real special parrot.. it understands six languages." And she says, "Well, I killed it for dinner and it didn't say nothin'.." (**All laugh**)

Phil: The natives in South America eat parrots all the time. You give a parrot to a South American and he'll be liable to cook it and eat it. They make real good eatin'.

Joe: We went on a cruise and at this one place they had some iguanas and they had a deer on a string. I asked about it being fresh and they said they don't have refrigerators. I said okay, that's our food.. that's dinner tomorrow. She was fascinated with the people down there and how industrious they were. We went down to an adobe making place and the man there had a wheelbarrow without a wheel. He just had a shovel and bring water in to make the bricks. It didn't take anything to make a livin'.

Phil: I used to watch them making those things in Texas. I grew up in Tennessee and Texas actually. My grandmother lived in El Paso, so I spent all my summers there. I watched them make adobe in the summer.

Joe: They used to bring us clay and mix it water and get it going real good. Then they'd put a little water and then lay it over these women's legs then shape it around the leg. Then they'd drill a hole and use a dull butter knife to cut around it and then they'd lift it up to lay it over there. And they were making tile for the roof! They'd have a skinny lady here and a heavy one over there.

Phil: Different sized tile for the roof.

Joe: I was pretty young in those days and I'd watch those girls.. it was pretty unbelievable. They make that tile pretty close to the site.

Winnie: Didn't that hurt their legs?

Joe: No, they put water on them and they'd do that all day long. One right after the other..

Phil: It was making them healthy too. They put all that paramagnetic clay on them.. they never got sick.

Joe: They'd stack it up all over there and bring in dung and roots.. anything they could burn and put it all on top of the tiles and bake them.

Phil: I'd seen indians do that in the jungles. The indians would do all sorts of strange things. The shaman too. I couldn't figure out what the shaman was doing.

Joe: The thing with these people of the jungles was feast or famine. All the food would come out at one time. All the fish would come at one time. There were periods for the elite. They hang these fish up and it would be very humid. They built fires around it and tried to smoke it, but the maggots would get in. And when you come in.. you're a special person and they want to do something nice for you.. and they pass out this rotten fish and you're supposed to eat it. I used to take this charcoal and eat it with the fish. And if you don't do that with those people..?

Marilyn: You've offended them.

Joe: You.. offend them. They done the very best for you. If they get out of their bed so you don't have to sleep on the ground you better sleep on that bed.

Phil: The Jewish people of Palestine had some kind of food. I guess you'd call it oatmeal or something. Bruggle they called it. God, I used to hate bruggle. I used to sneak it behind my back and put it in my back pocket.

Joe: The one that would bother me was, Poggi. These old men would be chewing corn and then spit it into this pot. If you were a special person, they'd run it through a piece of cloth and get some of that slime out of it. But to drink that stuff after it was fermented, it would uh...

Phil: Yeah, the taste of it would be enough to kill you..

Joe: ..it was enough to turn your stomach.

Phil: Yeah, it'd turn your stomach. I had to watch that in Israel. I'd have to sneak that into my back pocket.

Joe: As long as you went along with these people and you done the same thing they do, you'd be fine..

Phil: You're fine.. you're fine.

Joe: ..you could get a dart.

Phil: Yeah, you get a poison dart in your back. They wouldn't think of anything but of killing you.. that's for sure.

Joe: I think one of the things.. they can sense fear in a person. And they could also tell if you were sincere. If you had bad thoughts they knew it.

Phil: I lived with the headhunters for five years every summer. I spent five summers down with the Ashyari headhunters and got to know 'em real good.

Joe: I got out of there as quick as I could. They're getting real mean there because of these white people and these prospectors and this other stuff coming down there.

Phil: They were mean then because Ashyari headhunters didn't have any use for anybody. I was the only one really ever to go there and live with them. They'd have no use for anyone. They'd kill you just as soon as looking at you. Most people go in there with a gun or a knife.. even a pocket knife. I'd go in there totally unarmed and smiling. They'd look at me as if I was crazy, but then after a while they got to like me.

Joe: People that are crazy.. they treat them a lot better than they do with other people.

Phil: Oh sure. They probably thought I was crazy. I'd come in there laughing and talking and smiling.. I didn't have any weapons on me. I never had trouble with them at all.

Joe: They treat 'em like holy people even though they were crazy. People that's got afflictions or something.

Phil: I was real special to those people. I wrote a couple articles about them after the five years I spent with them. I could probably write a book about it now. There was one assistant shaman.. cause I got so close to the shaman that he got jealous. He was afraid of me and I knew he was afraid of me so I didn't have anything to worry about from him. He thought I was a greater shaman than the shaman.. he hated my guts, but he was afraid to put a poison dart in me. He could have killed me but he never did it. He probably thought that if he did, I'd come back as an eagle and kill him. They always had visions.. because if you take this drug that they had, uh..

Joe: Peyote.

Phil: It's like peyote.. it comes from a tree instead of a cactus, and it's just like it, but it's a different name. They take that drug and got these visions. I took it one night. I never had visions.. I just got sick to my stomach (laughs). I never took that again..

Joe: Well, we're facing some bad times. West Nile disease and things like that. I think the dragonflies we killed with the sprays.. things are out of balance.

Phil: That's what I'm going to try and stop when I get up there. It's a God thing for me to stop all that. When they give me the Congressional Medal of Honor they're going to be forced to hear to me.

Joe: When you start playing with nature and get things out of balance.. now, Rick and Sheri Herrera de Frey made a fortune, and became very

very wealthy raising ladybugs and raising little wasps and things like that.. they save the world.

Phil: Sure..

Joe: They sell them all over the world. They got a ten acre facility on the backside of the Catalina's called Arbico Organics.. I visit them once in a while. They're great advocates of you. You wouldn't believe it, you're books are lined up on the shelves. Sheri and Rick sell these bugs all over the world. I'm going to go back to them and try to them to get a hold of you and they'll probably call you. They got this West Nile, and dragonflies would do that or..

Phil: They got the cure for it right there.

Joe: Bats would be a good..

Phil: Dragonflies would be easier to rear and let them go in those areas where there's a problem with West Nile Virus.

Joe: How about Mad Cow disease. That's another one that's getting to be real bad. I think it's a lot worse than we realize now.

Phil: They can stop that immediately. That's just malnutrition in the cow.

Winnie: I thought it was the feed.

Phil: Well, it's in the feed because the feed's all chemical poisoning.

Winnie: It's all bad..

Joe: But if the cow had paramagnetics in it the immune system would take care of it.

Phil: Yeah, it would take care of it. You could put a couple tablespoons of ground up paramagnetic rock in the cow's water, which, of course, is why some cows with paramagnetics don't get sick. I noticed that a long time ago they don't get sick from these streams with the rocks, but the others were getting sick because they aren't protected. That water was not in contact with weak magnetic rock.

Joe: What if you took a ball like and screwed it right on where the pump comes in and filled it with magnetite, and then let the water go right through the screen before it got into the trough?

Phil: (**picks up the container with the paramagnetic rock and metal screw with the antenna as an example**) All you need is this on the collar of the cow.

Marilyn: I noticed now they have numbers clamped to their ears.

Phil: All you have to do is take that number which is probably metal. I don't know what it is if it's metal or maybe it's plastic.., and smear some Elmer's glue over it and sprinkle some of that paramagnetic rock in the glue..

Joe: It would be nicer if you had a möbius turned to the left and squeeze it right in there.

Phil: It's just as simple as taking that metal thing and putting some of that glue on it and sprinkle some of this on it and that would be the end of it. I'm gonna say all this.. I've got a chance of coming out and saying this and getting it out.

Joe: You're making it so cheap that nobody would be interested in it cause they couldn't get any money out of it.

Phil: That's why.. there'll be a guy getting a Medal of Honor saying it. I always wondered why I was getting it and now I know. God wants people to know about it. I gotta get up there and make a whole speech about paramagnetism. Everyone's gonna sit there and listen to it.

Joe: The world needs it. I can't believe that people haven't taken your book apart already. Remember I told you one time years ago..

Phil: I'm an entomologist. I'm not supposed to know anything about physics.

Joe: ..I got a job when I was a kid when I was about fifteen years old working for Coca-Cola before the war.. World War II. And they decided to raise the price on cases of bottles for deposit. And so they branded them. Remember I told you they branded a case with an iron brand? The ones that came back with a brand was worth more money than the ones that weren't branded. Mr. Martin was a pretty sharp businessman, but anyway he was making money on that too. My job was to make sure they were branded or not. I ended up making a little sensitive magnetometer that would tell me if the cases that went by were branded or not. I was getting enough magnetite from the burns to be able to measure magnetics. I learned to measure real low frequencies of metallics in that. But even when transferred from a hot iron to a piece of wood you could actually detect the paramagnetics.

Phil: The man who discovered that is a man named John Bindel. He was one of the greatest scientists that ever lived. He carved something out of wood one time.. he had made a CGS meter out of vacuum tubes.. a huge thing.. it wasn't as good as mine because he didn't have solid state physics back then. They had transistors by then, but it was a good enough CGS meter. He sat there watching and saw that this wood was jumping all around. He looked at it and looked at it then finally realized it had been branded with a copyright.. a little iron oxide transferred by the hot iron. Who ever had it in the lumber yard put his name on , so he'd know it was his lumber. That little bit of iron oxide from that iron made that piece of wood into a compass. It would turn around and point to north observing that there's a weak magnetism. He didn't call it anything.. he didn't know what it was. I got some of his earlier books. He's a mountain climber of which his first book was on mountain climbing, but he wrote six books. One of them was called "Heat is a mode of motion." That was his greatest scientific book ever written. But, they just sort of ignored him. That's where I learned most of what I know about infra red and nobody ever improved on it. Bindel was probably the greatest scientist that ever lived.

Joe: You're branding wood like that with an iron and leaving some of the paramagnetics in it, but what about the burnt carbon?

Phil: The burnt carbon is neutral because it's diamagnetic, so it's just like the wood. A lot of ranchers noticed when they branded a cow they had a lot healthier cow. A rancher told me that back when I was in agriculture. Branded cows were always healthier than the ones that weren't branded.. they had more energy because of the paramagnetic transference of the iron in the brand.

Joe: I have a real hard time branding women though. Would that make them healthy?

Winnie: Yeah, (laughs)

Phil: All you have to do is carry that in your purse.

Joe: Make a necklace out of it.

Phil: The best way is to get a quartz crystal and smear it with Elmer's glue then rub some paramagnetic powder until it gets into the pores of the quartz. It'll impregnate the little pores of the quartz and you'll never see it except under a microscope, of course, and it'll never wash off. Get some paramagnetism into it and hang it around your neck.. you'll never get sick.

Joe: You know how they put silver on coins now. They do it with implosion.. they blow it on. The silver is so thin when they make that little explosion over the coin, all the silver is pointed upward, then, it's aligned and it won't wear off. Plating is different because it's like sheets that'll peal away, but when you blow it on, such as with silver, it's more permanent. Now, why couldn't you do that with magnetite and quartz?

Phil: You can. If you wanted to make a fortune helping people to get healthy, you just blow silver onto a crystal..

Joe: Some magnetite.

Phil: With some magnetite onto a crystal.. you'll have a healing device.

Joe: That would all be under pressure.. that would be a piezo effect.

Phil: When I was into survival when I was behind enemy lines, I'd find a rusty tin can and scrape the rust into my water and I'd never get sick. I was eating all kinds of bad stuff.. you might pick water cress out of the stream but you wouldn't know if there was a cow up stream. You gotta be real careful but I never got sick. I just made sure I had paramagnetics in me.

Joe: If they were eating charcoal tablets with iron oxide in it that would be a beautiful..

Phil: Beautiful.. charcoal and iron oxide would cure for anything. If you put that into somebody's orange juice it would cure them of leprosy in a week.. which I did.. I cured 30-40 lepers when I was in the far east. They thought I was the greatest doctor there ever was

Joe: Almost like Jesus.

Phil: Yeah, the natives didn't care if the regular doctors liked me or not, they couldn't care less.. I cured people. The medical profession hates my guts and still do. The AMA won't even look at my stuff.

Joe: They can't profit on it.

Phil: No money in it. Anybody can go out and get granite or basalt.

Joe: Well, I fell in love with this iron oxide. I fell really in love with it.

Phil: This house is a pre manufactured house. There's no value in it. You can buy a house ten times cheaper

Joe: But you put magnetite in the walls.

Phil: Yeah, I did.

Joe: There's a man named Tom Brown who built a home in Oklahoma City. I shipped him the magnetite and he put it in the walls and oh man, he's got a beautiful house.

Phil: I just sprinkled a little of it in the plaster. And people say there's not enough there. And I say, "do you believe in transistors?" "Oh yeah I believe in transistors," they'd say. Well, you take a transistor, and it's a crystal, it's germanium and you drove it with four or five molecules of iridium arsenide and you got a transistor.

Joe: Just a coating.. just a splattering.

Phil: You got a transistor.

Joe: They take a piece of quartz crystal just like that and they apply a coat of gallium arsenide.. just a tiny coating of it and it'll collect sun and turn it into electricity. A solar cell.

Phil: That's what a solar silver cell is. It's real easy to make a silver cell. That's what I was doing in World War II. I don't say this when Winnie's around because she doesn't want to hear about the IRA, but the IRA wanted to kill me. Not only did I have a parrot that could tell me that they were coming, but I had a little radio receiver in my pocket that was run by a rock. It would start buzzing in my pocket and they couldn't get close to me. If the parrot didn't say something, just a tuned circuit run by a piece of basalt would save me.

Joe: A quartz radio set?

Phil: A crystal set using a rock crystal that would work like a quartz crystal, but with basalt.

Joe: I can't talk about it with Winnie because she doesn't like how I talk about the IRA. I'll probably write a book about it.

Joe: You got a dozen books in ya.

Phil: I got eighteen books already. I need to write one on terrorism. I already got it written but I need to send it to Acres.

Joe: Bruce Halstead was worried about this. Halstead said we're so easy to poison. He said that if these terrorists pick up on these and transfer these frequencies of poison into the things we think are safe, like aspirin, they wouldn't even have to break the seals.

Phil: They won't do it though. I found out that God's got a program that will disable stupid people. Terrorists could read all my books. I've got all the frequencies waves of poison in my eighteen books, but they're too stupid to do it.

Joe: You think God built in this protection.

Phil: God has built stupidity into evil. So there's no problem. Otherwise I'd be dead. If terrorists weren't stupid I'd be dead. God, I parachuted behind German lines.. I got away from the IRA easy..

Marilyn: Dr. Deal, you know, says that thoughts you think are the most important thing. They're extremely strong.

Phil: If terrorists weren't stupid, I'd be dead.

Joe: I always thought that God just took care of drunks, little children, and people like me.

Phil: I believe He does... Like you and me.

Joe: I shouldn't be alive. I mean I should have been killed a half-dozen times.

Marilyn: It sounds like Dr. Callahan here should have been dead more than a dozen times.

NOTE: Both men have averted death several dozen times in their lives each.

Phil: You're probably not as healthy as I am. I don't know if you're overweight..

Joe: I am overweight. I just eat too much.

Phil: I have a high rate of metabolism. I probably eat as much as you do, but I metabolize it. It just gets burned off. I never sit still for long.. I'm sitting here now, but I'm usually up doing something.

Marilyn: Lately he's been spending too much time sitting on the couch.

Joe: I've been a couch potato.

Phil: You gotta be careful what you eat. Start eating right and put paramagnetic dust in your water. You make one of these paramagnetic containers and carry it in your pocket and it'll keep you from over eating.

Joe: Suppose I take some crystals and I put some frequencies in there and I take a Viagra and squeeze it between some rocks and leave it under pressure?

Phil: Probably get stronger. That's a lot of work just to make it.

Joe: I'm thinking about that Viagra. I might be making that.. I think you can get the same frequencies..

Phil: You can take Viagra which is a good medicine that puts out real good frequencies obviously and put it one of these things and you'll live about ten years longer.

Joe: You know what Viagra is? It's Nitrous oxide.

Phil: Is that all it is?

Joe: That's all it is. It's as simple as zeolite in Johnny Cat kitty litter. It absorbs the gases. For Viagra, they put together and press it. That's all it is.

Phil: Some smart guy thought it up.

Joe: I think that the guy that thought it up was in Hot Springs Arkansas. All he did was bubble nitrous oxide in water and called it Happy Hollow water. All these old men would come around and drink the water and what it did was help the blood circulation. Nitrous oxide, we've known that for years, but then kitty litter absorbs the gases like ammonia.. it pulls it right in. We've known that when Pfizer bought the place down there in Bowie, Arizona, that makes zeolite. We went down there the last time and they had locks on the place. You couldn't even get in.

Phil: That's kind of funny 'cause my father retired in Hot Springs because he used to believe in that water, but he died from cigarette smoking. My mother, however, lived to ninety. She didn't smoke, of course.

Joe: I sold a lot of this iron oxide to Reynold's Metal Company and they took it up to Area fifty one in Nevada. They used it for screening around radiation.

Phil: Yep, that'll stop radiation. I suggested that to them. That's why this country can't grow so much.. this area measures about two or three thousand CGS and that's why we grow so much plants around here, but in other deserts don't grow anything because there's not enough paramagnetic rock.

Joe: Sedona has about three thousand CGS. but the strongest I've measured is in Central Arizona right under Black Mountain and that's where I get that stuff I'm getting.

Phil: That's probably getting ten thousand or more.

Joe: Nineteen thousand.

Phil: Nineteen thousand. That Black Mountain is the sacred mountain to the Navajo Indians.

Joe: Sure is, but anyway that whole mountain is iron. There's something about the sunlight. Iron will run ten, fifteen, and twenty percent. But then when it works it's way down.. there's something about the sunlight. This stuff has been washing through the washes for years and years and years and the sunlight enhances it.

Phil: Right. Paramagnetism stores up sunlight. This container is storing up sunlight in this room here. With the fan going up there you got an electrical energy too, so it's really strong in this room.

Joe: So, the movement of the fan creates eddies or currents in the air that transfers magnetic energy.

PART THREE

The interview continues with Phil and Joe in the room Winnie has just cleaned.

Phil: I don't know, there's something about names that men don't pay much attention to. Women remember names a lot better than men. I think what happens to names is that you don't have nothing to hold on to so they're just floatin' around out there. So, they're harder to remember.

Joe: I remember I got into trouble when I was a kid one time, I was trying to remember things and I used to put anchors to them. The teacher was talking about Columbus and I said, "1492 Columbus sailed the deep blue sea.." Anyway what I'd done is combine the wrong words.. "two" for the ocean blue, and three for "sea". It didn't work out.

Phil: It didn't work that way.. two instead of three..

Winnie and Marilyn: Bring the bird..

Joe: Bring the bird in.

Phil: Oh, that bird can't stand being by itself. Birds.. parrots are social birds. Because they're social, they live in groups they cannot stand.. he'll fly out. I kind of watch him when he flies because he might run into something.

Joe: My dad had a parakeet.. he thought a lot about that parakeet.

Winnie: (**To the parrot**) There you go.

The bird flies over to Phil and Joe sitting on the couch.

Joe: Oh, he wanted to go see you.

The bird actually settles on Joe's shoulder and remains there during the rest of the interview

Phil: He likes you.

Winnie: He might go on his shirt

Marilyn: That's okay if he poops on his shirt.

Joe: He knows who's boss. Boy, he's got a big eye. Well, it looks like I got me a bird here.

Phil: He's happy to sit there, but he doesn't want you to pick him up. you got a one tract mind birdie.

Marilyn: He wants to be in control there.

Joe: Well he is.

Phil: He does.. he want's his photograph taken now.

Joe: Well, that bottle is something I'm going back to.

Phil: You got the right idea. It's actually pretty good the way it is.

Joe: Well, you know, Dr. Ricketts used to tell me that same thing and so did Ralph Bergstresser, "Joe, no matter what it is, you're going to try to monkey with it. If it's working, don't go any further. You'll sell a lot more Fords or Chevrolets than a Cadillac."

Phil: Yeah, everyone knows a Ford or Chevrolet works just as good as a Cadillac. They aren't interested in Cadillacs. The only people that own Cadillacs are people that want to show themselves off. Most people can only afford a Chevrolet.

Joe: You know. I don't care much for cats.

Phil: I don't either.

Joe: But, I'll tell you.. everywhere I go the cats will jump in my lap.. the cats will come up to me because they know I don't care much for them. There's nothin' there to like.

Winnie: We always had cats on the farm at home.

Phil: I didn't like them.

Winnie: I know, I had them to keep the rodents and mice out.

Phil: Yeah, but they're not like dogs.

Joe: Now, I love dogs.

Phil: Cats are opportunists. They're just with you because they know they're going to get fed.

Joe: And they're so damn arrogant.

Phil: Cats are arrogant, there's no question about it.

Joe: Anyway, I'll carry this a little further and get a few things to you. I'm looking forward to you finishing your book.

Phil: I've got two books. It's not so hard to write a book.

Joe: I'll be tinkering with this for a while.

Phil: All this stuff I have in my books.

Joe: I'll try to get a hold of Shandra and see if I can get Christopher Bird's last deal and get that to you.

Phil: Christopher Bird was a really great friend of mine.

Joe: He really loved you too. He really did. I never seen him a single time where he didn't ask if I'd seen you. I really didn't know that much about you. He liked Sedona. He said anytime I'd like to come up and see him I could come up and see him. He didn't like coming down to that desert.

Phil: Sedona is a beautiful area, but those houses up there.

Joe: Well, what they've done is they got the price of everything so high. Even a trailer lot up there is over a hundred thousand dollars.

Phil: It'll probably keep it from getting over crowded. That's for sure.

Winnie: Probably is crowded.

Joe: A lot of rich people.

Marilyn: There's a lot of rough land so they can't get close together which keeps them scattered.

Phil: It's pretty scattered and as long as they keep them separated out. It's like around here you don't even notice the houses. There's a lot of open land still.

Joe: I'll try to get with Mr. and Mrs. Frye at Arbico and see if they can start raising dragonflies to wash out the West Nile.

Phil: If they're really worried about West Nile that's the way to cure it. All they'd have to do is raise enough of them, but that's not hard to do.

Joe: Dragonflies, they like a little wet environment, but they also like paramagnetics too.

Phil: Sure. A wet environment and paramagnetics and you can raise them by the millions. The West Nile virus will be gone in a year.

Joe: And, you think the way to cure Mad Cow disease is to wear magnetite around the cows necks.

Phil: Hang one of these around the necks and you won't have to worry about the Mad Cow disease anymore. The disease is partly caused by the insecticides, but the way to protect them is with paramagnetics. There's so much of the insecticides around now that the best way to protect the cow is with weak magnetic fields. They even found DDT in the Antarctic.

Joe: Yeah, I heard that. Even on the little American side.

Phil: It takes thirty years to break it down so it'll take another hundred years.

Joe: And yet, if you expose it to paramagnetics and sunshine, it's broken down almost instantly.

Phil: There's none around here and you can't even get a reading of it because the ground is full of paramagnetics.

Joe: You take that little deal right there and sprinkle some around the school yard and you won't find a trace of it eight hours later.

Phil: There wouldn't be any DDT in the schoolyard.

Joe: Electrified hydrocarbons they call them.

Phil: Strangely enough the schools that have paint over on the green and the asphalt parking lots are highly paramagnetic. It's hard on the bones if you trip and fall, but it's a lot better with blue grass or the asphalt.

Joe: So, the old paved asphalt roads are healthier than the concrete?

Phil: Sure, just look at the weeds that grow up along the edges. The weeds are full and tall. If I ran out of paramagnetic rocks, and that happened to me in Ireland, I just went out and chipped some asphalt off the road and put it into one of those containers.

The bird is picking at Joe's face. It had been playing with Joe the whole time.

Winnie: He's really checking you out.

Phil: He's checking you out alright. He's trying to figure out your facial beard. It's a lot like mine.

Marilyn: He's thinking, "How come there two of you all of a sudden?"

All laugh

Joe: Well, I get along with kids, dogs and now birds. It's people I have trouble with once in a while.

Phil: I never had any problems with kids. Two girls followed me around.

Winnie: I'm not going to say anything.

Marilyn: Were you one of them Winnie?

Joe: You picked the right one, Winnie.

Marilyn: You got the cream of the crop.

Phil: I got the cream of the crop. I think God picked the right ones for us.

Joe: I think I made the right choice too. I got the same one I started with. But, ah, all my kids have been lucky. I had one that her husband got on drugs. One got divorced and she's remarried now to a lawyer. And I got a good granddaughter out of that. We only had one divorce in all our family. It was the drugs and it bothers me real bad.

Marilyn: The kids turned out good. We have daughter and son in laws with good grandchildren.. they're not all perfect, but close enough to perfect.

Joe: We have one that has a little trouble reading. And yet, he has good grades, but has to work hard.. real hard.

Winnie: He wants to learn because he studies.

Marilyn: He's got a mother and father that are willing to work with him and encourage him. He's pretty good now that I think of it. It was when he was younger that they had to work with him.

Marilyn and Winnie continue talking about their children and family while Joe and Phil carry on with their conversation.

Joe: I've got fungus on one hand and my toes after going down to South America that I have never been able to get rid of.

Phil: You take some of that paramagnetic rock and rub it over your finger nails and hands.

Joe: Well, you're getting close to your nap time and so we'll wait another year before we see each other. I think you should put pamphlets out. Nobody reads volumes anymore, but if you put out quick to read books, or pamphlets, you'd sell. I think where your big deal is when you talk to people in short bits. Bruce Halstead wrote these big thick books that were three inches thick. As time went on, he wrote these little pamphlets that sold. He was making money selling the pamphlets.

Phil: I think I got something over here (**Phil gets up to look for his pamphlet**)

Phil: I found one of the pamphlets. That's about the Virgin of Guadalupe.

Joe: I've never seen this one.

Reproduction of the Tilma of the Virgin of Guadalupe

Phil: The Catholic Church put this out. They didn't sell much and there not many left. They're out of print.

Joe: I'll buy this one..

Winnie: No, we have some left. There's about three or four.

Joe: I never read much about the Virgin of Guadalupe. An artist friend of mine, he passed away, he made millions of dollars on religious paintings.

Phil: That's visible and that's infra red. It's got no drawing under it. Any water color painter draws a picture first before they paint. Also, the face isn't pigment. It's diffraction radiation. It's white limestone and light is refracted from it so it looks like a face. It's an incredible picture.

Close up of the Virgin Guadalupe reproduction

Joe: I never saw this book before.

Phil: No you won't. It's out of print now too.

Winnie: They were never for sale honey.

Phil: I never sold anything. Acres sells them.

Joe reads a quote from the pamphlet 'The Tilma Under Infra-Red Radiation'..

Joe: "Let me learn the lessons you have hidden in every leaf and rock."

Phil: It's an old Indian prayer. It's the oldest Indian prayer. Indians didn't write though.. that was written when..

Joe: The ancient Turks didn't have a written language. I have a lot of Indians that visit me and some of them stay quite a while. Willie Whitefeather comes through once a year just to stay with us. Now, he wrote a book on survival and it actually saved some kids lives. They remember what they read about Willie and it got a national write-up.

Marilyn: It's written for kids, but it's got information for adults.

Joe: Now, I don't understand all the things about infrared and far infrared. Far infrared is what's catching the attention of the astronomers.

Phil: (**demonstrates wave forms using his finger**) Light is a wave length this long, infra red is that long and far infrared is this long. Instead of little short waves, they get longer and longer.

Joe: When this is ingested in your body, you're getting internal heat. And, it's almost like getting a temperature to get rid of a virus.

Phil: You're getting rid of radiation without heating the body up.. the heat will kill you beyond a hundred and six degrees temperature.

Joe: Did you do a book on the cloth like this?

Phil: It's in a book. It's a chapter in a book. I did the work on the shroud and I did the work on the Virgin of Guadalupe. I'm the only man in the world that's touched both of them. After I did the work on the Virgin they invited me to Italy to do the work on the Shroud of Turin. I'm going to write a whole book about it.

Joe: You really believe that they were inspired.

Phil: Oh yeah. The shroud of Turin is quite a shroud for certain. There's no question about it. Nobody could have painted it.. it would be impossible. It's a radiation image which was formed by high energy. When Christ rose from the dead it was from high nuclear energy that actually photographed the shroud.. made an impression. When you open it up, his back is on one side and his head is on the other side. It's a piece of cloth that folds over from the back to front.

Joe: The imagery is paramagnetic.

Phil: Sure. It's diamagnetic cloth and paramagnetic iron oxide. What happened, because typically they didn't take baths, there was a lot of soil.. he dragged that cross a long ways getting the soil all over his body which had the iron oxide. As he died, there was a burst of energy and all that iron oxide was dragged out impregnating the shroud. I actually ran experiments on that. I would take a piece of damp cloth and put some iron oxide on it and the iron oxide would migrate to wherever there would be electrical energy. I took pictures.

Joe: When people die, there is a burst of energy that is measurable in grams. The French made a lot of studies on this, but they could never capture that. They put domes over it and glass over it. They did everything in the world to catch that weight.

Phil: That's because it's different energy. Neutrons have no charge. They have no minus and no plus. It can be measured with certain instruments, but the neutrons, you can't control it.. you can't store it. To measure something you have to store it first. Neutrons are going right through us now. Which is the bad thing about never leaving your house. It cuts down on the neutrons.

Joe: Neutrons leave us with certain transferrable energy?

Phil: Yeah, sure you need it.

Joe: Neutrons will go right through a block of lead.

Phil: You'd die if you had any in your body. You get it from the sun of course, but they go right through you. In one experiment that costs six hundred million dollars, they filled a cave full of water and it finally got to a point where they could actually measure the neutron. The neutron had to go through a couple miles of water.

Joe: They did this under the mines in Japan. Something happened with the neutron tubes and there was an implosion. It costs millions of dollars to replace it. They replaced it immediately.

Phil: It collapsed the original tubes and they had to make them stronger.

Joe: Whenever they were taking pictures of this they could catch a neutron going through the water, but they always had to have a man on the camera. If they had a camera without a brain on it they couldn't get a picture. But, a camera running by itself wouldn't catch it. They could never understand why.

Phil: You had to have a brain process it. Well there is no computer to process it.. your brain's the computer. The brain understands neutrons. The brain receives and broadcasts the right frequency that understands the neutron to capture the image.

Joe: (passionate) I could never understand why would people.. well like you and other people.. I'm a nobody. I'm not an educated person. Why do I talk to.. why will people talk to me like that and tolerate me. Teller and Halstead.. we become all friends. And you..?

Phil: Tiller was a down to earth man too.

Joe: You know what I'm saying about these people.. I'm not in their class! I'm like a parasite living off very important people.

Phil: Oh, yes you are. It's like my father used to say that he never went to college, but he ended up being a brigadier general for a week in the war. I went from corporal to sergeant to captain to lt. colonel in a year. He did the same thing.. like father like son.

Joe: I've often wondered about it. The people that talk to me and spend time with me and.. I knew a geologist, Dr. Pye, he was a teacher at the University of Arizona...

End Tape

Dr. Philip Callahan has not yet received a Congressional Medal of Honor. His hope was to voice the truth about our planet and our health. It is assumed his voice would have irreversible damaging effect to the cartels that run the industry of ill health, corruption in agriculture, as well as prevent the detrimental effectiveness HAARP has on the environment and earth's inhabitants. Paramagnetism is an integral key to saving this planet as we see it being dismantled at an exponential rate. You will not find Phil Callahan's name in such seemingly reputable information web depositories such as www.wikipedia.org. The Wikipedia page on paramagnetism, although he invented the term, not only doesn't mention his name, but doesn't list the common terms that reference to paramagnetic characteristics such as "iron oxide, ferrous oxide, pink granite, granite, basalt," and all of the items of information shared in this interview. Not Philip Callahan, nor his eighteen published books on entomology, infra red radiation, paramagnetics, natural phenomena, and the many scientific papers, are noted on wikipedia.org. This is one clear example where information is suppressed at the level of mass information and educational venues that would otherwise damage the powerful industry that educates them. Both Philip Callahan and Joe Blankinship share a strong desire to educate our youth.

www.ingramcontent.com/pod-product-compliance
Ingram Content Group UK Ltd.
Pitfield, Milton Keynes, MK11 3LW, UK
UKHW041940190726
13854UKWH00004B/1700